Easter by Heart

How to Memorize the Gospel Stories of the Resurrection

Learn One Verse a Day
For the Season of Easter

Books by Heart™

Bill Powell

BLUE VINE

First edition 2013.
Printed in the United States of America.

Easter by Heart, version 1.1.

Published by Blue Vine Books.

To order this and other **Books by Heart**™ directly from the publishers,
please visit: BlueVineBooks.com

Cover design and typesetting by Wineskin Media: WineskinMedia.com

ISBN-13: 978-0615823904
ISBN-10: 0615823904

The cover of this book was laid out using *GIMP*.

The text was composed in *markdown*, edited with the text editor *emacs*,
and converted to various formats with *pandoc* and *calibre*.

The text of this book was set in Lato and Palatino, using the LaTeX macros
and LaTeX packages, especially *memoir*, with the TeX typesetting engine.
The output PDFs were previewed with the PDF reader *evince*.

These programs are professional, open source, and free.

Cover artwork includes elements courtesy of:

lostandtaken.com
spiritsighs-stock.deviantart.com

The ornaments throughout the book are in the public domain, provided
courtesy of: openclipart.org.

This book includes the **Books by Heart**™ lessons, version 1.2. These
lessons have been adapted for this text, to help you memorize the Resurrection.

For Mike and Joe

But the Paraclete,
* the Holy Ghost,*
whom the Father will send
* in my name,*
he will teach you all things,
* and bring all things to your mind,*
*   whatsoever I shall have said to you.*

Jn 14:26

In this book,
    you will learn
the Resurrection of Christ,
    from the Gospel of John,
        by heart.
You will hear and feel the rhythms,
    imagine the scenes,
        and renew your memories.
By the end of the Easter season,
    you'll know these words by heart.
But your memories of the Resurrection
    will have only begun.

Contents

ix

This Easter Season, Learn the Resurrection

Easter: Where Christ Gets Interesting

How long do you celebrate Easter? A day? A morning? Did you know you're supposed to get a full **fifty days**? The Easter season lasts for **seven weeks**!

By contrast, Lent only lasts for *forty* days. Yet hordes of Christians struggle and groan through six weeks of Lent, shout with relief on Easter Sunday, and then ... forget the whole thing before they finish the Easter candy.

It's like we scrimp and save to buy a red Mercedes, then let it rot in the garage after a single joyride. Easter is a *season*, not a single day of egg hunting and festive hats.

Let's face it. This whole crazy Christianity thing hinges precisely on whether one particular man did or did not have the power to come back to life.

Modern culture has gravitated toward Christmas, the other end of his life. Christmas does turn the world on its head, as the omnipotent Creator becomes an impotent newborn, hiding in a cave. But we already love babies and birthdays.

Funerals? Not so much. Even the Crucifixion doesn't quite change our view of funerals. Good people get slaughtered every day.

But Easter turns every funeral you've ever seen inside out and upside down. Easter makes the *personal* implications suddenly get interesting.

Change the World. Party This Easter.

How did our cultural conversation about Christianity ever degrade into catfights about sexual ethics? I don't think this would happen if we actually celebrated Easter. What if every spring, millions and millions of people openly partied for weeks because *a dead guy broke out of his grave*, and they fully expected to see him again and *live forever*?

Everything would change.

Everything *can* change. What's our problem? Either we don't really believe in life after death … or … we just don't think about it much.

It would be easy to veer off into a depressing appraisal of our collective faith, hope, courage, trust, and other forms of love. But that's not what I'm here for. I want to help you grab the low-hanging fruit.

Celebrate Easter by Learning the Story

Action follows thought. Before we assume our hearts are stone cold, let's try *thinking*. You need to sow seeds of thought if you want to reap joy. And you can only think with what you remember.

This Easter season, this book will show you how to learn the actual words of the story of the Resurrection by heart. If you learn just **one new verse each day**, you'll know the **entire Resurrection story from John** by Pentecost.

During the Easter season, you can learn one verse each day from the last two chapters of the Gospel of John. By Pentecost, you'll know the entire Resurrection of Our Lord by heart.

The math is almost perfect. There are 50 days from Easter to Pentecost, and 51 verses in the Resurrection chapters of John.

Built-in Daily Time With Christ

Learning these verses will help you think new thoughts, and actually celebrate that God plans for you to live forever.

All kinds of prayers have spiritual value. But it's a special experience to *say the words* of the Bible, to tell those stories. You can think about what you're saying, and you're always saying something new.

Also, you'll say these words every day. That's part of learning by heart. Don't panic! This daily repetition doesn't take long, and it doesn't last forever.

Besides, these daily recitations become built-in daily meditation time. Learning the Easter verses isn't just a *goal*. The actual *process* of daily renewal and thought becomes a way to celebrate the season.

All the Details You've Been Missing

As you learn the Easter stories of John (and in future years, the Easter stories from the other Gospels), you'll be surprised at all the *details*. There's much more to the story than the empty tomb.

Those few weeks after Christ's Resurrection are so mysterious. He keeps surprising them, following some plan that's never explained. When the women get to the tomb, he's already gone. Why? Why deputize an angel? We don't know. We just know the details. That's what happened.

But then he meets Mary Magdalen anyway — and she *doesn't recognize him*. And then, instead of going straight to the cowering apostles, he takes a long walk towards Emmaus with two second-tier disciples, one of whom isn't even named. (Note: I love the Emmaus story, but it's not in John, only in Luke, with a brief reference in Mark.) He sets their hearts on fire, vanishes, and then, after they run all the way back to the upper room, he disdains the locked door and joins them.

Even then, he doesn't stay. It's unclear how often they see him over the next few weeks. Finally, what does Peter do? He goes fishing. It's so realistic it hurts. Has he hit rock bottom, reverting to his old job, as if nothing had happened? Or is this just how he passes the time, waiting for the Paraclete? We don't know. But that's the detail.

And though I love the idea of learning all the last precious words of Christ in these final chapters, my favorite moment may well be right here. Jesus fills their nets to bursting, one last time. Peter swims to shore, and he finds that his crucified and risen Lord, who made the blind see, the deaf hear, and the lame walk, who cleansed lepers and bound devils and made corpses sing again, who has conquered death and will shortly fly to the clouds to take the throne of the universe ... he's just made breakfast.

It makes me want to cry. Who would have dreamed a God like this?

And how do we keep losing him? How do our mental images keep blurring and shifting and melting, until words like *God* and *Jesus* and *Christ* conjure only pathetic flickers of boredom or guilt?

The details await us. We can draw the crisp lines of clear, true mental pictures. Phrase by phrase, scene by scene, we can weave the real, living Christ into our thoughts. This Easter season, we can bring Christ to life.

How This Book Will Help You Learn the Resurrection

This book includes two major aids to learning the Resurrection this Easter, plus a **bonus feature**.

First, you get the **verses of John 20 and 21**, type-set as **rhythmic stories**. Although you could learn the verses from any Bible, this book uses a **visually memorable** layout. Instead of blocks of prose, you see these words with rhythms that move like poetry. This gives each verse a more unique look, and also helps you **speak** and **hear** the verses with rhythm. They become much easier to remember.

Second, you get the **Books by Heart™ lessons**. These lessons will show you, step-by-step, how to remember a long text like John 20 and 21. These lessons form the core of this book. They've also appeared in other books in the series, such as *Lent by Heart* or *Christmas by Heart*.

The bulk of these lessons are the same in every book in this series, because all these books focus on memorizing the same kinds of texts. But in each book, I adapt certain examples and discussions for the particular text we're learning. In this book, we'll focus on the Resurrection narrative from John.

You can read the whole book at once, but the lessons are also designed so that you can read one lesson a day. You start learning one new verse a day right away, and the lessons gradually tell you what you need to know as the days pass.

As a bonus feature, I've also included **rhythmic verses** for the **Resurrection stories from the other Gospels**, as well as the **Pentecost story** from Luke.

If you'd rather learn a different Resurrection narrative this Easter, you can make that choice.

Or, for future Easters in the years to come, you can **use this book again** to learn other Resurrection narratives. You'll find these stories at the back of the book.

I use the Douay-Rheims Challoner version for the all the Scripture in this book. This old translation will probably remind you of the famous King James version. Although the DRC presents some challenges, it also has features that make it a great choice for memorizing. I explain these features in a later chapter.

Let's begin with a slow, thoughtful reading of John 20 and 21.

The Story of the Resurrection from John

Here are the fifty-one verses you'll learn this Easter. They tell the story of Christ's Resurrection, from the twentieth and twenty-first chapters of the Gospel of John.

You'll be coming back here every day, so while you're here, **bookmark this page.** Keep one bookmark here, at the beginning, and move another bookmark forward each day to your new verse.

For now, as you read these stories for the first time, **don't think about memorizing**. Just read. Many words and phrases will be familiar, but expect to be surprised.

John 20
Easter Morning
John 20:1

Mary Magdalen comes to the sepulchre

And on the first day
　　of the week,
Mary Magdalen cometh early,
　　when it was yet dark,
　　　　unto the sepulchre;
and she saw the stone
　　taken away from the sepulchre.

She ran, therefore,
　　and cometh to Simon Peter,
and to the other disciple
　　whom Jesus loved,
　　　　and saith to them:
They have taken away the Lord
　　out of the sepulchre,
and we know not where
　　they have laid him.

Peter and John come to the sepulchre

Peter therefore went out,
　　and that other disciple,
　　　　and they came to the sepulchre.

And they both ran together,
　　and that other disciple did outrun Peter,
　　　　and came first to the sepulchre.

And when he stooped down,
    he saw the linen cloths lying;
but yet
    he went not in.

Then cometh Simon Peter,
    following him,
and went into the sepulchre,
    and saw the linen cloths lying,

And the napkin
    that had been about his head,
not lying with the linen cloths,
    but apart,
        wrapped up into one place.

Then that other disciple
    also went in,
who came first
    to the sepulchre:
and he saw,
    and believed.

For as yet they knew not
    the scripture,
that he must rise again
    from the dead.

The disciples therefore departed again
    to their home.

Mary Magdalen meets the Risen Jesus

But Mary stood at the sepulchre without,
    weeping.
Now as she was weeping,
    she stooped down,
        and looked into the sepulchre,

And she saw two angels in white,
    sitting,
one at the head,
    and one at the feet,
where the body of Jesus
    had been laid.

They say to her:
    Woman,
        why weepest thou?
She saith to them:
    Because they have taken away
        my Lord;
and I know not where
    they have laid him.

When she had thus said,
    she turned herself back,
        and saw Jesus standing;
and she knew not
    that it was Jesus.

Jesus saith to her:
    Woman,
        why weepest thou?
            whom seekest thou?

She,
   thinking it was the gardener,
     saith to him:
Sir,
   if thou hast taken him hence,
tell me where thou hast laid him,
   and I will take him away.

Jesus saith to her:
   Mary.
She turning,
   saith to him:
Rabboni
   (which is to say,
     Master).

Jesus saith to her:
   Do not touch me,
for I am not yet ascended
   to my Father.
But go to my brethren,
   and say to them:
I ascend to my Father
   and to your Father,
to my God
   and your God.

Mary Magdalen cometh,
   and telleth the disciples:
I have seen the Lord,
   and these things he said to me.

The Risen Christ Comes to the Disciples
John 20:19

Jesus comes to the disciples in the Upper Room

Now when it was late that same day,
    the first of the week,
and the doors were shut,
    where the disciples were gathered together,
      for fear of the Jews,
Jesus came and stood in the midst,
    and said to them:
      Peace be to you.

And when he had said this,
    he shewed them his hands
      and his side.
The disciples therefore were glad,
    when they saw the Lord.

He said therefore to them again:
    Peace be to you.
As the Father hath sent me,
    I also send you.

When he had said this,
    he breathed on them;
and he said to them:
    Receive ye the Holy Ghost.

Whose sins you shall forgive,
    they are forgiven them;
and whose sins you shall retain,

they are retained.

Thomas meets the Risen Jesus

Now Thomas,
    one of the twelve,
        who is called Didymus,
was not with them
    when Jesus came.

The other disciples therefore
    said to him:
        We have seen the Lord.
But he said to them:
    Except I shall see in his hands
        the print of the nails,
and put my finger
    into the place of the nails,
and put my hand
    into his side,
        I will not believe.

And after eight days again
    his disciples were within,
        and Thomas with them.
Jesus cometh,
    the doors being shut,
and stood in the midst,
    and said:
        Peace be to you.

Then he saith to Thomas:
    Put in thy finger hither,
        and see my hands;

and bring hither thy hand,
    and put it into my side;
and be not faithless,
    but believing.

Thomas answered,
    and said to him:
My Lord,
    and my God.

Jesus saith to him:
    Because thou hast seen me, Thomas,
        thou hast believed:
blessed are they
    that have not seen,
        and have believed.

Jesus is the Christ

Many other signs also did Jesus
    in the sight of his disciples,
        which are not written in this book.

But these are written,
    that you may believe
that Jesus is the Christ,
    the Son of God:
and that believing,
    you may have life
        in his name.

John 21
Jesus at the Sea of Tiberias
John 21:1

Simon goes fishing

AFTER this,
    Jesus shewed himself again to the disciples
        at the sea of Tiberias.
And he shewed himself
    after this manner.

There were together
    Simon Peter,
and Thomas,
    who is called Didymus,
and Nathanael,
    who was of Cana of Galilee,
and the sons of Zebedee,
    and two others
        of his disciples.

Simon Peter saith to them:
    I go a fishing.
They say to him:
    We also come with thee.
And they went forth,
    and entered into the ship:
and that night
    they caught nothing.

Jesus sends them a huge catch of fish

But when the morning was come,
    Jesus stood on the shore:
yet the disciples knew not
    that it was Jesus.

Jesus therefore said to them:
    Children,
        have you any meat?
They answered him:
    No.

He saith to them:
    Cast the net on the right side of the ship,
        and you shall find.
They cast therefore;
    and now they were not able to draw it,
        for the multitude of fishes.

That disciple therefore
    whom Jesus loved,
said to Peter:
    It is the Lord.
Simon Peter,
    when he heard that it was the Lord,
girt his coat about him,
    (for he was naked,)
        and cast himself into the sea.

But the other disciples
    came in the ship,
(for they were not far from the land,
    but as it were

two hundred cubits,)
dragging the net
    with fishes.

Jesus makes breakfast

As soon then
    as they came to land,
they saw hot coals lying,
    and a fish laid thereon,
        and bread.

Jesus saith to them:
    Bring hither of the fishes
        which you have now caught.

Simon Peter went up,
    and drew the net to land,
full of great fishes,
    one hundred and fifty-three.
And although there were so many,
    the net was not broken.

Jesus saith to them:
    Come,
        and dine.
And none of them who were at meat,
    durst ask him:
        Who art thou?
knowing
    that it was the Lord.

And Jesus cometh and taketh bread,
    and giveth them,

and fish in like manner.

This is now the third time
    that Jesus was manifested
        to his disciples,
after he was risen
    from the dead.

Simon and John

John 21:15

"Simon son of John, lovest thou me?"

When therefore they had dined,
    Jesus saith to Simon Peter:
Simon son of John,
    lovest thou me
        more than these?
He saith to him:
    Yea, Lord,
        thou knowest that I love thee.
He saith to him:
    Feed my lambs.

He saith to him again:
    Simon, son of John,
        lovest thou me?
He saith to him:
    Yea, Lord,
        thou knowest that I love thee.
He saith to him:
    Feed my lambs.

He said to him the third time:
    Simon, son of John,
        lovest thou me?
Peter was grieved,
    because he had said to him
        the third time:
            Lovest thou me?
And he said to him:
    Lord, thou knowest all things:
        thou knowest that I love thee.
He said to him:
    Feed my sheep.

Amen, amen I say to thee,
    when thou wast younger,
thou didst gird thyself,
    and didst walk
        where thou wouldst.
But when thou shalt be old,
    thou shalt stretch forth thy hands,
and another shall gird thee,
    and lead thee whither
        thou wouldst not.

And this he said,
    signifying by what death
        he should glorify God.
And when he had said this,
    he saith to him:
        Follow me.

Will John die?

Peter turning about,
 saw that disciple whom Jesus loved
  following,
who also leaned
 on his breast at supper,
and said: Lord,
 who is he
  that shall betray thee?

Him therefore when Peter had seen,
 he saith to Jesus:
Lord,
 and what shall this man do?

Jesus saith to him:
 So I will have him
  to remain till I come,
what is it to thee?
 follow thou me.

This saying therefore went abroad
 among the brethren,
that that disciple
 should not die.
And Jesus did not say to him:
 He should not die;
but, So I will have him
 to remain till I come,
  what is it to thee?

The world could not contain the books

This is that disciple
    who giveth testimony of these things,
        and hath written these things;
and we know
    that his testimony is true.

But there are also many other things
    which Jesus did;
which,
    if they were written every one,
the world itself,
    I think,
would not be able to contain
    the books that should be written.

You're going to learn all that by heart. Let's get started!

Books by Heart: Resurrection

Now we begin the Books by Heart™ lessons, which will show you an easy method for learning these verses by heart.

You may have already read a similar version of these lessons in another book in this series, such as *Lent by Heart* or *Christmas by Heart*. But in this book, I've adapted certain examples and discussions for John 20 and 21.

You don't have to read this whole book on Easter by Heart! Instead, you can do **one lesson per day**. Read the first lesson, say the first verse, and then it's up to you how quickly you read the other lessons.

Speaking Out the Verses

Every time you say a verse, you want to:

- **Speak out**: Speak **loudly** and **slowly**, with **rhythm** and **expression**.

- **Take it in**: As you speak, **see** the words as they are written, **hear** the words you say, and **feel** the **rhythms** and the **shapes** of the words on your tongue.

- **Experience**: Let the words lead you to **imagine the scene** in this **story**.

Seem like a lot to remember? Don't worry, we'll be going over all this in detail. You'll always see critical points more than once.

In this first lesson, you'll learn how to **speak out** the Gospel. Speaking out is the crucial first step. You have to speak a verse before you can **take it in** and **experience** it.

Speak Out

You're used to reading silently. But in ancient times, they were used to reading out loud. Words were *spoken*. And the first step to learning these stories by heart is to **read the verses out loud**.

Read the verses out loud:

- **loudly** and **slowly**

- with **rhythm** and **expression**

Loudly

How loud? **Loud enough to hear yourself.**

Don't mumble. When you mumble, the words only happen inside your head.

You need to be loud enough to *hear* your own words, as if someone else were talking to you. Hearing the words will activate additional mental processes, and lead to stronger memories.

You always want to **activate as many different kinds of learning as possible**. Each kind of learning has its own set of **mental connections**. The more connections you make, the stronger your memories.

Slowly

Don't rush! When you're first learning new verses, speak slowly. Not *painfully* slow, but a little slower than you usually talk.

In normal speech, we slur past common words. Here, you want to **pronounce every sound in every word**.

Rhythm

The Bible has rhythm! Unlocking these rhythms makes the verses both come alive and stay in your mind.

As I mentioned earlier, I've typeset these verses like a **poem**, instead of the usual prose paragraphs. Here's the first verse:

And on the first day
   of the week,
Mary Magdalen cometh early,
   when it was yet dark,
      unto the sepulchre;
and she saw the stone
   taken away from the sepulchre.

You're looking at one of the best-kept secrets about the Bible. **The Bible has rhythm.**

Oral Culture

The Bible was written in an **oral culture**, a culture that largely depended on the spoken word. Human speech has a natural, loose rhythm. In an oral culture, speakers make these rhythms even stronger.

They organize their thoughts into words and phrases that play off each other, back and forth, rising and falling. Their audiences *expect* these rhythms, listen for them, and remember them.

In our culture, we associate rhythm with *entertainment*: nursery rhymes, popular music, rap. Advertising jingles.

Our serious work *avoids* rhythms. Doctors don't want to sound like Dr. Seuss.

But oral cultures *depend* on spoken rhythm for serious work. Jesus preached in rhythm. The Gospel writers composed with rhythm.

Free the "Verses" Back Into a "Poem"

You want to **speak** these verses with **rhythm**.

Almost every Bible translation imprisons these verses into long, solid columns of compressed text. But why do we call them **verses**? Don't verses mean a **poem**?

Poems never translate well. Most rhythm, like rhyme, is lost in translation. But if we listen to our Bible translations, especially an older translation, we can still find the **back-and-forth rhythm** of the phrases.

The first modern scholar I know of to unlock these Bible rhythms was Marcel Jousse, a French priest in the early twentieth century. In 1925, his book *The Oral Style* revealed that beneath the prose of the Gospels, even in translation, the phrases rise and fall with strong rhythms.

Back and Forth Rhythms

Let's look again at our first verse, John 20:1. Normally, that verse would look like this:

And on the first day of the week, Mary Magdalen cometh early, when it was yet dark, unto the sepulchre; and she saw the stone taken away from the sepulchre.

But I've freed these words into a more natural, back-and-forth rhythm:

And on the first day
    of the week,
Mary Magdalen cometh early,
    when it was yet dark,
        unto the sepulchre;
and she saw the stone
    taken away from the sepulchre.

Do you hear how the phrases interlock? One phrase rises, creating tension. The next phrase falls, resolving the tension.

and she saw the stone ... taken away from the sepulchre

Where did she see the stone? Taken away from the sepulchre

This rise and fall, question and answer, is much stronger in some places than others. But even the more prosaic sentences can be broken into short phrases and spoken with rhythm.

Speak With Rhythm

Every verse in this book has been set with rhythm. As you read, use the layout to help you see and speak these rhythms. You'll usually see **couplets** and **triplets**.

The first line of this **couplet** rises, creating tension,
    The second line falls and resolves the tension.

The first line of this **triplet** rises, creating tension,
    The middle line begins to fall,
        But only the last line resolves the tension.

Sometimes, you'll see a set of four lines. I'm not sure Jousse would approve of this. He only talked about groups of twos and threes. But sometimes, it seems to me that a line really "introduces" a triplet:

And someone says, in a rising tone,
    "I'm saying something that rises even further,"
        And only now does the tension begin to fall,
            And this fourth line completes it.

You May Find Better Rhythms

So what rules have I used to break up these verses into groups? Here's my secret method: whatever sounds good.

There *isn't* any secret method. If you find a better rhythm for a cluster of verses, change it! And let me know! (bill@howtoremember.biz) I'd love to improve future editions.

Skip the Verse Numbers and Headings

You'll notice that, just now, when I showed you the rhythmic verse, I didn't include the verse numbers or any headings, such as "Mary Magdalen comes to the sepulchre". Although that information is helpful, I do *not* think you should memorize it. For me, it's enough to know which book and chapter I'm memorizing from.

As you saw when you read John 20 and 21 earlier, I do include headings and some verse numbers in the full selection. But I don't suggest memorizing them.

If you wanted to know the chapter and verse, the best way would be to *say* "John, chapter twenty, verse one" before that verse. But even if you shortened this to "John twenty one," it would sound ridiculous, like a computer printout. It would disrupt the story, and kill the rhythm.

Expression (These Words Are *Alive*)

At first, speaking the Bible with rhythm may seem unnatural. Even disrespectful.

Why? Because we in the English-speaking world have this bizarre tradition of the **reverential monotone**.

Ditch the "Reverential Monotone"

Think about church. Unless you're very lucky, your lector "proclaims" the readings with less expression than your GPS. You'd get more drama from R2D2.

Somehow, we've gotten the idea that the Bible needs a *special* voice: a *dead monotone*.

But what's so reverent about a monotone? These words are alive, and so are you. A Bible is just a sacred suitcase to carry those words from Christ to you.

Sadly, the words had to have all the expression and intonation hacked off so they'd fit in the suitcase. Your job is to unpack them, and try to get them back to normal.

The monotone is not normal. The monotone is dead. When our cultural air is thick with the conviction that the Bible is a dead old distant book with nothing to offer, a monotone is the worst possible choice.

The monotone is also the worst possible choice for remembering.

Let the Words Live

Freeing the rhythms helps the words live. But you want to go even farther. You want to **tell the story**.

Think about telling a story to a friend. Or reading a story to a child. The expression comes naturally. It flows from what's happening in the story.

Tell the story. Expression will come naturally.

Now Speak Your Verse

That's all you need to get started! This has been a long first lesson, but don't worry. Soon you'll be focused on learning verses, not learning *how* to learn them.

Read the verses out loud:

- **loudly** and **slowly**

- with **rhythm** and **expression**

Throughout the rest of the day (or tomorrow, if it's already bedtime), **read the first verse out loud again every few hours**. Don't worry about memorizing it yet. Focus on speaking it well.

Your Memorizing Plan

Now that you know how to **speak out** a verse, let's back up and look at our overall plan for memorizing. Many people offer different methods for memorizing Scripture. I want you to understand why my *Books by Heart* approach is simple, easy, and natural.

A Daily Verse

The core idea is simple: every day, you learn one new verse, and repeat the verses you've already learned.

Learning one new verse every day, and renewing what you've learned, doesn't take long. We're talking **fifteen minutes** or so, spread throughout the day.

It may not seem like much. But this small effort gives you powerful leverage. The words of the Gospel are potent. They're like strong magnets, attracting thoughts and feelings that would otherwise rush by. Bit by bit, you will think differently.

Besides, the verses add up fast. By Pentecost, you'll know John's whole story of the Resurrection, from Mary Magdalen coming to the tomb to Christ's final words to Peter by the sea of Tiberias.

Why Only One Verse a Day?

You may assume that memorizing is difficult. Or, you may be surprised that you're only learning one verse a day. Can't you do more?

Eventually, yes. But if this is your first time, you're training a new skill. Your mind is *extremely* susceptible to the patterns you set right from the beginning. If you tried to start out memorizing two or five or ten verses a day, you would inevitably start to rush, and then feel burdened and overwhelmed. The whole experience would sour.

Instead, focus on getting this one verse *right*. It's like push-ups. Ten push-ups with correct form will do much more for your body than twenty sloppy attempts.

Also, memorizing requires *review*. By only adding one new verse a day, your daily renewal won't take too long.

When you complete this project, if you want to learn more, you can try learning two new verses a day for a month. And then three. And so on.

But for now, stick to one. Master the art.

Why You *Can* Memorize

Maybe you're wondering whether you can *really* memorize even one new verse a day. Perhaps you're constantly reminded of your "bad memory" as your car keys vanish and critical mail evaporates.

Guess what? **I promise that your memory is *excellent*.** How do I know? **Because you can read.**

Think about it. If your memory were actually *broken*, would you be decoding these squiggles into words, linking them to *sounds*, snapping them into phrases and sentences, making the impossible leap into kaleidoscopes of *meaning* — all at hundreds of words per minute?

I don't care if you take reading for granted. I don't care how they graded you in school. You can read. Your memory is amazing. Period.

Whatever "memory" problems you have are due to *technique* and *habit*. These are precisely the skills you'll learn to improve in this book.

Even the most amazing tool will fail if you don't know how to use it. You're going to learn *how* to remember these verses.

Your Daily Routine

You'll only need to spend about **fifteen minutes a day** on this project.

Even better, you'll spread this time in bits throughout the day. Every day, you will:

- Repeat the verses you've already learned, all together, as a **series of stories**.

- **Learn** your **new verse**.

- Throughout the day, **repeat** your **new** verse **three or four times**.

- If you're having trouble with any older verses, repeat these too. You'll be surprised at how easily you can fit these short reviews into the crevices of your day.

- At the end of the day, **repeat all** your verses again **once**, including your new verse.

You might prefer to learn new material at the *end* of the day, sleep on it, then review throughout the next day. That's fine.

This daily routine is the core of learning by heart.

If you miss a day, pick up where you left off.

We'll explore this routine in more detail later. This is all you need to get started.

Stories, Not Memory Tricks

I keep saying "verses", but the Gospels are a series of **stories**. Stories are much easier to think about and remember than individual verses.

If you've used other memory books, you know there's a wide variety of memory tricks out there. I've tried most of them. Sadly, much of this advice actually makes **memorizing verses more difficult**.

If this book saves you from even one standard mistake, it will pay for itself many times over.

For instance, have you heard about "mnemonics" or "memory palaces"? Some books suggest using these visual memory tricks for anything you want to learn, but I disagree.

For this project, **you don't need any wacky memory tricks**. You won't need to imagine any crazy pictures or funky memory sentences.

Instead, you'll learn how to make the **verses themselves** a **memorable experience.** You'll unlock their power with **rhythm**, **expression**, and **imagination**.

Mnemonics aren't inherently harmful. If you want to memorize your credit card number, mnemonics work great. But they're not the right tool for memorizing texts. I'll explain why further on.

For now, let's move to the next step in memorizing. As you speak a verse out, you also **take the verse in**.

Take the Verses In

You've learned how to **speak the verses out**:

- Speak **loudly** and **slowly**

- With **rhythm** and **expression**

Now you'll learn how to take verses *in* as you speak them.

When you **take verses in**, you:

- **See** the words and phrases

- **Hear** the words and phrases

- **Feel** the **rhythms**

- **Feel** the **shapes** of the words on your **tongue**

See the Words

The first step to taking in the verse is to see the words. This seems obvious. But when I say *see*, I mean *intense attention*.

Reading this book, you've already seen and understood thousands of words. But *how* have you seen them? Right now, close your eyes, count to ten, and try to call up images of these pages.

What did you see? Anything? At best, you probably got a fleeting glimpse or two.

Does this mean you have a "bad" memory? No. Your mind did exactly what you've trained it to do.

It slurped the *meaning* from the words as quickly as possible. Why didn't you keep mental snapshots of every page, like Sherlock Holmes, Monk, or Shawn Spencer?

For the same reason you didn't keep the can the last time you opened some tuna. You didn't need to. Your mind has better things to do than hold onto every page you read, and it knows it.

But now it's time to take those mental snapshots. You want to train your mind to "photograph" each verse.

That may sound impossible. But think of all the pristine mental images you *can* call up. (Corporate logo trivia, anyone?) Learning to capture verses simply takes practice and good technique.

"Photographing" Each Verse

Intend to see perfectly. Tell yourself that you can and will remember this verse exactly as you see it on the page or screen.

Look with intense **attention**. Normally, your gaze races down sentences. Instead, look as if you were looking at a painting. See these words as a unique visual image, not mere symbols.

Focus on **details**. Don't try to "photograph" the entire verse at once. Study it phrase by phrase. Notice the font, the spacing, the place on the page. All these little details seem to come together in our minds like the tiles of a mosaic.

As you try to recall the verse later, **refresh** your memory as needed. If you forget something, look at the verse again. Fill in the gaps.

Over your first few recitations, you'll remember some bits, but not others. Make the effort to remember. But if you don't get it after a few seconds, look at the book. There's no point in waiting. Get those missing mosaic tiles. Your goal is an *effortless* memory.

True, if you check too quickly, you may train yourself to always need the book. You may even trick yourself into thinking you can't memorize at all. But this is a balance you'll have to work out for yourself. Even if you only remember one or two more words each time, you're moving in the right direction.

Be patient with yourself. This may be a brand new skill for you. If you have to keep checking, don't worry. Gradually, you'll learn how to see clearly.

Perfection Is Easier Than "Almost"

Should you try to learn the verses *perfectly*? Yes. Because perfection is easier than "almost".

I know this because I have "almost" memorized hundreds of verses. I've memorized the entire Gospel of Mark — *almost*. When I learned this
Gospel, I was using a different system, so I didn't
learn them perfectly. Today, I can say many verses
perfectly. But I'll say many verses with a slight para-
phrase, or the occasional missed word or phrase.

You might think, so what? What's a mistake
here and there, if you still basically know the whole
Gospel?

For years, I thought so too. Then I realized something. Every time I hit a patch I wasn't perfectly sure
about, I had to *hesitate*. I had to consider two or more
possibilities for what came next.

Not only did this waste time and cause anxi-
ety, but it made the whole memory *shakier*. Blurrier.
More likely to fail next time.

These days, I'm "polishing" my Mark memories.
I know that whenever I hit a verse where I'm uncertain, I need to check the text and repair this memory
right away. When I skip this, I make more work for
myself. My mind knows that I'm not sure about this
verse. Next time, my hesitation will be the same, or
worse.

Instead, I need to check the text and make that
repair. *Now.*

You Remember That You Forget

Back when I was settling for "almost", I was actually
memorizing the *entire experience* of not quite knowing the verse.

Your memory is that amazing. You can memorize
that you have trouble memorizing something.

The stronger this flawed memory becomes, the harder it becomes to ever learn the verse correctly. You have too much mental baggage, half-memories of all the different versions you concocted in your mental thrashing. It's a mess.

By contrast, when you know a verse perfectly, you *know* you know it perfectly. It's easy. No more stress. You get a flash of exactly how the verse looks or sounds.

It's easier to learn a verse perfectly than to almost learn it. The key is to correct your uncertainties right away by checking the book.

The Context of the Story

Many books and websites offer a "daily verse," isolated from anything else. In the first edition of *Christmas by Heart*, I did the same thing myself, and showed each day's verse on its own page. They looked so nice, with all that lovely white space.

But you won't get good results if you try to memorize a verse all alone on a page. Instead, read and reread each verse in its place in the full story. Seeing the verse as part of the story, rather than alone on a page, puts the verse into **context**. As you read and reread each verse, this unique context will help you remember.

Hear the Words

Just as important as *seeing* each verse is to **hear the words**. As I said earlier, you should always hear yourself saying these words.

You should physically **hear yourself** saying these verses.

When you say verses out loud, you're literally talking to yourself.

We "talk to ourselves" all the time, but most of this conversation happens inside our heads. For memorizing, that isn't enough. You want to hear your own voice.

Hearing activates more parts of your mind and memory than the usual mental self-talk. Remember, the more ways you connect to these verses, the better you'll remember them.

Feel the Rhythms

We've already talked about speaking the **rhythms in the Bible**. These rhythms can change your whole experience of these stories.

But the rhythms go beyond speaking. When you speak with rhythm, you also *hear* rhythm. You even *feel* it. You can *feel* the pause, the tension, the resolution.

You don't need constant awareness of these rhythms. Mostly, you sense them without realizing it. But sometimes, especially when you're starting a new verse, or the passage is difficult, you can help clarify the memory by paying attention to the feel of the rhythm.

Feel the Shapes of the Words in Your Tongue and Mouth

You can also **feel the shapes of the words** in your tongue and mouth.

Try it. Go to the full story at the back of the book, and read yesterday's and today's verses together three times.

- First, as you would normally read aloud.

- Second, as you learned to speak earlier: **loudly** and **slowly**, with **rhythm** and **expression**.

- Third, paying attention to **forming each word** with your **tongue, lips, and mouth.**

Did you feel the difference?

When you feel the shapes of the words, you get **clarity**. It's like a muffled voice becoming clear.

As with feeling the rhythms, you don't need to be constantly aware of these sensations. But they're another layer of experiencing these words. If you give some attention to shaping the words, especially when you're first learning verses, it can help etch the words into your mind.

These shapes help make words and phrases *unique*. The more unique they are, the better your mind can remember them.

Renew Your Verses

As you learn more about memorizing, remember that **daily renewal is core of learning**.

> Repeat your new verse three or four times today.
>
> At the end of the day (or tomorrow morning), repeat all the verses you've learned as a series of stories.

Remember, focus on **speaking each verse out** ...

- Speak **loudly** and **slowly**

- With **rhythm** and **expression**

... and **taking each verse in** ...

- **See** the words and phrases

- **Hear** the words and phrases

- **Feel** the **rhythms**

- **Feel** the **shapes** of the words on your **tongue**

Try to say these verses without looking at the book. But if you get stuck, reread them. Remembering should *never* be a struggle.

Learning these verses should not be a self-test! We're doing the exact **opposite of a test**. On a test, you're punished for finding the right answer outside yourself. Here in real life, what matters is *knowing*. If your memory isn't clear yet, read the book and clarify it. Once you make clear memories, remembering will be almost effortless.

Experience

So far, you've learned how to **speak the verses out**:

- Speak **loudly** and **slowly**
- With **rhythm** and **expression**

And also how to **take the verses in**:

- **See** the words and phrases
- **Hear** the words and phrases
- **Feel** the **rhythms**
- **Feel** the **shapes** of the words on your **tongue**

Now you'll learn how to **experience the verses** in your **thoughts** and **imagination**.

Move Through the Words into Thoughts

Imagining is both the simplest and the most mysterious aspect of learning these stories by heart.

It's simple because, in theory, we all know how to imagine. At the very least, we dream every night.

But the mystery of imagination sometimes bewilders me. Imagination is so *personal*. We hardly have the language to articulate what happens inside our heads.

The obvious meaning for "imagination" is a mental *image*, like a picture or movie. But what we do with these verses can be much more complex.

Here's the critical point: you want to **move through** the **words** into **thoughts**.

Move through the words into thoughts.

These thoughts can include:

- scenes and sensations

- places

- feelings

- memories

- meaning

Scenes and Sensations

Obviously, whenever you can, you want to imagine the *scene*. What's happening?

You can see images and hear sounds, like you're watching a movie. But use your other senses too. Taste. Smell. Touch.

You can experience *any sensation* you can remember. We hear songs "in our head", but you can also smell the crisp morning air of the garden, and feel the warm breath of Christ as he gives you the Holy Spirit.

Places

Think of your sense of *space*, of a place opening around you. Your imagination, like the real world, is three-dimensional.

When you use your sense of space, you can put yourself *into* the scene. You can experience it as if it's happening to you.

When Jesus calls the disciples to breakfast on the shore, don't imagine a tiny holy card. *Look around*. Even if you're in your bedroom, you can *be* outside, by the sea, with a fresh wind coming off the water and birds calling over the waves.

Or, you can ground your scenes in actual places that you know. Where's your safest place to hide and lock the door? Throw that deadbolt, huddle next to a friend — and then suddenly, *He's there*.

Feelings

How does the scene make you feel? What about the people in the scene? Can you feel what they're going through? Emotions can shock you with their intensity.

Memories

Think about your life memories. Has anything like this ever happened to you? Linking to a scene from your own life creates a powerful resonance.

Meaning

Not every verse describes a scene you can visualize. That's fine. Abstract thought is important too. A verse can inspire a whole train of thought.

Some memory guides place a huge emphasis on visual memory, and I did so myself when I was starting out. I needed this emphasis. I found out my visual imagination was incredibly more powerful than I'd assumed.

But not *all* thinking has to be visual.

This list of possible thoughts only scratches the surface. You can think about these verses in as many ways as you can think.

Imagining Is a New Skill

The problem? Thinking takes work. For most of us, imagining is a new skill, and that means effort.

Our default response to reading is the easy route — identification. Identification is the great hazard of memorizing.

We read that first verse:

And on the first day
    of the week,
Mary Magdalen cometh early,
    when it was yet dark,
        unto the sepulchre;
and she saw the stone
    taken away from the sepulchre.

And we think, "Oh, right, Mary Magdalen. The stone. The sepulchre. Identified. Done. What's next? I've heard this story *so many times*."

This ordinary reading happens on a superficial level. We don't *imagine* anything. We don't *think* much at all, unless something happens to strike us.

And that's fine. Ordinary reading is quite useful for ordinary purposes.

Ordinary reading is like walking through the forest. You don't need to be aware of the unique contours of every tree. You just need to keep an eye out for berries (and bears).

Our minds are fantastically equipped to be constantly awash in seas of information, and attract only the essential bits. We excel at this. If we didn't, we would starve to death trying to make breakfast.

Most of what you read doesn't matter. Your mind plucks the essentials, and forgets the rest.

Now, however, you're suddenly asking your mind to remember *every word*. This is a new skill.

You've become an aspiring artist. You've hauled your easel out into the forest, and you have to learn to *look*.

Like any new skill, deliberate imagining takes practice. You need to slow down and *think*. Branch out. What can these words lead you to? What can they *connect* to?

Imagining Is Connecting

Look again through that list of ways to think about the verses. Notice how they're all **connections**.

You imagine the garden by *connecting* this idea to the *sensations* of a real garden: the smell of flowers, the chill of the early morning air.

You imagine the *shock* and *excitement* and *relief* of the apostles by *connecting* to your memories of your own emotions. Have you ever *almost* lost someone? Have you ever had a friend you thought you'd never see again? Remember when you realized they were going to make it? With a tiny bit of thought, those emotions flood back.

Or what about that last, miraculous catch of fish? John takes time to show us the boat "dragging the net with fishes", and poor Peter hauling the huge net to the land. Remember the last time you had to pull a rope or lift a couch? This story might be *too* easy to enter.

We often think of memorizing as a special, arcane skill. But memorizing, like imagining, is ultimately connecting. You think, "I want to tell the story of when Christ conquered death," and that concept *connects* both to the actual words of the story and to the vivid thoughts you've crafted.

Why do you forget things? Because you lose connections. The data doesn't get *erased*, as if you're a hard drive. The data gets *lost*. It sinks into the murky seas of your subconscious. That's why you can forget someone's name, but as soon as you hear it, *you remember it*. The name was in your head, but you couldn't find it.

This leads to a powerful idea. When you connect the words of the verses to vivid thoughts like scenes, places, memories, and feelings, those connections don't only help you experience the verses. They help you *remember* them.

Imagining is **connecting**.

Memorizing is also **connecting**.

What do you connect to? **Your own experiences.** You connect new material to what you already know.

Imagining Brings Delight

Your own experiences are incredibly vivid. In fact, the word *vivid* comes from the Latin word for "life". Your experiences *are* your life. The more you connect verses to your own experience, the more you literally make them *come to life*.

Let's take a simpler example. Read this sentence:

John ate a cookie.

Normally, this sentence would not detain us. "John" is probably a little boy. And we all know what eating a cookie is. This kind of filler clogs the arteries of many a mediocre bedtime story.

But suppose I actually walked into the room with a platter of cookies. Your *favorite* kind. Freshly baked.

In real life, there's nothing boring about a platter of fresh cookies. It doesn't matter that this incident isn't movie material. It doesn't matter that you've already eaten thousands of cookies over the course of your lifetime. When you *smell* your favorite kind of cookie, and take that bite ... life is good.

Now here's the crazy part. As you read this, is your mouth actually watering? In a way, you just *did* eat a cookie.

I know this isn't *The Matrix*. I'm not trying to blur the crucial distinction between imagination and real life. I am trying to show you how closely they intertwine. Your real life is far more *available* to you, as memories, than you realize.

You can sit here and experience eating your favorite kind of cookie. You can *relive* the smell, the taste, the warmth, the feel of the food in your fingers and your mouth.

(Maybe I should have eaten breakfast before I wrote this lesson.)

I keep saying "your favorite kind," because that helps point you to *specific* experiences. We don't sit down and eat the Platonic ideal of a cookie, like that poorly drawn character in the children's book. We eat an oatmeal cookie, or a chocolate chip cookie, or a banana nut cookie, or a peanut butter cookie, or a gingerbread cookie, or a molasses cookie ... they are each *different*. Unique. Precious.

You can only remember eating a *specific* kind of cookie. If you don't know which cookie you're eating, you're still thinking abstract thoughts *about* eating cookies. You're not smelling any warm cinnamon or tasting any peanut butter.

If you do succeed in remembering actual tastes and smells — you'll know! It's a *jolt*. You will *feel* these things again. It's so different from abstract thought.

I'm afraid we need to wrap up this cookie meditation. Perhaps you're getting impatient to enjoy a celebratory Easter cookie in real life.

But here's the takeaway. If you wanted to, you could relive all these delightful memories as soon as you read:

> John ate a cookie.

That one sentence could be enough.

"Unpacking" the Cookie

And you could go even further, beyond this sugar-free approach to enjoying dessert.

If you have small children or grandchildren, you could remember how they look when you give them a dessert, how happy you are to make them happy.

You could think about how children enjoy food, with no fear or guilt. On the other hand, you could consider how this innocence has led to an epidemic of childhood obesity and diabetes.

You could find yourself musing on the balance between enjoyment and temperance, on the search for delight that does no harm ... suddenly John is exploring a forest, making a snowman, feasting on grapes in the middle of winter ...

I'll stop my cookie exegesis. But sometimes I think I've found the secret to why so much language in Scripture, and the texts and stories from other ancient cultures, are so sparse and succinct. They had no TVs. No one did their imagining for them.

They didn't need painstaking descriptions and telling details before they slowly began to imagine a net bursting with fish. You just said that "although there were so many, the net was not broken," and their minds exploded into cinematic fireworks.

I can't prove this, of course. But I'm fairly sure.

And the delights of imagination are entirely unique. They are *creative*. What is creativity, anyway, but making new connections?

Move beyond **identification** to **connect** with your **experiences**. These connections can bring intense, creative **delight**.

Your New Daily Routine

Over the last few lessons, you've learned the essential skills you'll need to remember these verses.

- **Speak out**: Speak **loudly** and **slowly**, with **rhythm** and **expression**.

- **Take it in**: As you speak, **see** the words as they are written, **hear** the words you say, and **feel** the **rhythms** and the **shapes** of the words on your tongue.

- **Experience**: Let the words lead you to **imagine the scene** in this **story**.

You've also begun to memorize new verses. And you're renewing what you learn, using the **daily routine** I showed you earlier.

Now I'd like to explore that routine further. Why does it work? How can you fit this time easily into your schedule, and remember to do it?

Spaced Repetition and "Smart" Intervals

If we were going to memorize a longer text, such as an entire Gospel, I would teach you about "spaced repetition" and "smart intervals". In spaced repetition, you take advantage of how the brain functions to time your reviews as efficiently as possible.

The basic idea is simple. At the *beginning*, when you first learn material, you have to repeat it many times. This repetition seems to convince the brain that, unlike the rest of the torrent of information engulfing you each day, this material is worth holding onto.

After these early repetitions, you slowly leave more and more space between your repetitions. Before long, you're waiting weeks, months, and years between repetitions.

You can use free computer flashcard programs like Anki to track each bit of material automatically. This brilliant system of "spaced repetition" can help you retain huge amounts of material in your mind.

A Simpler Method: Repeat Every Day

However, spaced repetition also requires a certain amount of planning. I'll explain that method in upcoming books which involve memorizing more material. For the stories in this book, the overhead isn't worth it.

Instead, let's keep things simple. Every day, at least twice, recite all the verses you've learned so far. Say them together, as a series of stories.

Every day, at least twice, recite all the verses you've learned so far. Say them together, as a series of stories.

You won't have to do this forever. For now, since we're "only" learning about two chapters' worth of verses, it's easy and quick to just recite it all every day during Easter.

At the end of the book, I'll explain how you can maintain these verses into the future, without having to say them every day.

Say Recent Verses More Often If Needed

Ideally, twice a day will be enough for all the verses you've already learned. But you may find that you're uncertain about one or more verses, especially the verses you only learned yesterday or the day before.

No problem. At the start of the day, when you say all the verses you've learned, pay attention to when you hit your first uncertain verse.

Normally, the next step would be to learn your new verse, and then repeat only that new verse an extra three or four times throughout the day.

But when you hit an uncertain verse, *start there* and recite up to and including your new verse throughout the day.

These extra recitations will only take a minute or two, but they'll make all the difference. Again, you start with the earliest "shaky" verse that you had trouble with, and recite through to today's new verse. Easy.

Strengthening Uncertain Verses

Let's say that you've learned from John 20, verses 1 to 6. Today, you plan to learn verse 7.

But when you start reciting from verse 1, you find that you're unsure about verse 4.

You learn verse 7, as planned. Then, throughout the day, you recite verses 4 through 7 (not just your new verse 7), three or four times.

In the evening, you recite the whole thing again, from verse 1 up through verse 7.

Your Daily Verse Routine

Once more, here's the full daily routine:

- First, in the morning, say all the verses you've already learned.

- If any verses are uncertain, refresh your memory from the book. Note the earliest uncertain verse that you have trouble with.

- Then, study today's new verse. Repeat the new verse several times as you learn it.

- Every few hours, start with the earliest uncertain verse, and recite straight through to your new verse. Do this **three or four times** altogether.

- Later in the day, say all the verses again. (They make a perfect extra bedtime story.)

Crafting Your Routine

Learning these verses depends on **daily time**. It doesn't take much time, but it does need to be done every day. You face two obstacles:

- Finding time to say the verses

- Making it a habit (actually saying them)

Finding Time to Recite

Can you say these verses while you're doing something else? That's the first place to look, because you won't even have to change your schedule.

Do you already take a walk every day? Or have a time when you read and relax? Or put your kids to bed? How about morning or evening prayer?

Learning and reciting verses won't merely "fit" into these slots. These new habits improve them.

For instance, prayer. With a little thought, learning and reciting verses can easily become a prayer.

Bedtime Stories

If you have kids, get ready for major synergy.

When I put my kids to bed, I read them their bedtime stories, and then I say some verses. If I had *replaced* the stories with verses, there might have been a mutiny. But they're perfectly happy to get the verses as *extra* stories.

By now, if I don't say verses, they're disappointed. Even better, they've learned huge chunks of my verses just by *listening*. When I hesitate, they sometimes pipe right up.

In fact, they often want to interrupt and ask questions. We can wind up launching into a mini-seminar. If I tried to *schedule* "Bible discussion time" during the day, I could easily waste a lot of effort trying to pry out some interest. But because it's bedtime, and because when Papa leaves, that's it for the day, suddenly all this Scriptural interest blossoms unbidden. Sometimes I have to ask them to stop interrupting.

You're going to tell these stories anyway, for your own practice. With a little planning, you can make your storytelling enrich your family's lives.

Making a Habit

Habit is crucial. You've probably heard that it takes around **three weeks** to form a new habit.

Hook to Your Existing Habits

The easiest way to start a new habit is to **hook it to something you already do every day.** For instance:

- Getting up and going to bed

- Breakfast, lunch, and dinner

- Morning and/or evening prayer

- Putting the kids to bed

Can you say these verses when you first get up, and right before you go to bed? How about before or after a meal? If you already pray every day, definitely consider including a recitation.

A Simple Daily Routine

- When you wake up, say all your verses, and learn your new verse.

- Before or after each meal, start at your earliest uncertain verse, and recite up through your new verse.

- In the evening, after your prayers (or reading a bedtime story), say all your verses.

Get Someone to Pester You

You should also get someone to pester you. The grownup word for this is "accountability". But Jesus didn't tell any parables about "accountability." He did tell a parable about a widow driving an unjust judge crazy.

In my case the kids take care of this. "Do you have any verses tonight, Papa?" they ask, in that special kid voice that is hopeful, hesitant, and (sometimes) infuriatingly irresistible.

Track Your Progress Like Seinfeld

Remember Jerry Seinfeld? Supposedly, an aspiring comedian once asked him the secret to success. According to the story, Seinfeld told him that:

- A comedian needs to be as funny as possible.

- The only way to get funnier is to practice writing jokes.

- So you need to write jokes **every day**.

- And the best way to make sure you do this every day is a **huge chart on your wall**, with a **year's worth of daily boxes**.

- Every day, if you write your jokes, you put an "X" in the box.

- Pretty soon, you have a chain of X's.

Success, according to Seinfeld, is simple. "Don't break the chain!"

I've tried this "Seinfeld chart," and let me tell you, it's the most effective habit-building tool I've ever seen.

From where I write, I can glance over and *see* my charts, one for each habit I'm trying to form or maintain. (For instance, writing this book.) Look at all those X's! Pow! Instant affirmation doesn't get any sweeter. All those X's are things I've actually *done*, not goals or "To Do" items.

So use a chart. No excuses. I've made a free chart for you at **EasterByHeart.com**. Download it, print it off, and tape it somewhere prominent. Put a marker, preferably bright red, within arm's reach of where you hang it. Not a pencil. You want to see these marks from across the room.

And don't just use that parish monthly calendar you get for free. It's critical to see *several months* at once.

Daily Recitation Times + Chart = Habit

We've boiled this new habit down into two steps:

Step 1: Plan precisely when you're going to say your verses each day. Don't bother about *times*. Focus on *hooks*. Which daily habits will you hook your verses to?

Step 2: Go to **EasterByHeart.com**. Print the daily "Seinfeld chart". (Disclaimer: No, this chart is not officially endorsed by or associated with Seinfeld in any way.) Tape the chart to the wall in a place where you can easily see and mark it.

With your daily routine planned, and a chart to track your progress, you'll soon find you have a habit.

Bible Stories

In the last lesson, you learned how to craft your personal **daily routine** for saying verses. Have you tried hooking your recitations to any habits yet? If any of your decisions didn't work, don't worry. Today's a new day. Try again, or try something else. You can always tweak.

Gospels as Stories

We're used to dividing the Bible into chapters and verses. But nobody applied this system to the Gospels until centuries after they were written. When people first heard John, they heard a series of *stories*.

Today, **biblical storytellers** have brought back this focus on the Gospels as stories. Scholars such as David Rhoads and Tom Boomershine have written books with titles like *Mark As Story* and *Story Journey*. There's even a Network of Biblical Storytellers.

When they meet, the festivities include tellings of whole books of the Bible.

Jousse taught me to find the Bible rhythms. These folks taught me to find the Bible stories. When I first started memorizing Scripture, I still focused on chapters and verses. Now I understand that the earlier unit of *story* is far more natural, memorable, and enjoyable.

The word "story" here is broader than what we usually mean (a tale with a protagonist and a beginning, middle, and end). In this context, a "story" is basically a series of verses that hang naturally together. It could be the conversation between Jesus and Nicodemus in the third chapter of John, or the first section of the Sermon on the Mount.

Remembering Stories

How do you divide verses into stories? There are no hard and fast rules.

For John 20 and 21, I have four major stories:

- Easter morning

- The risen Christ comes to the disciples

- Jesus at the sea of Tiberias

- Simon and John

Our basic unit of learning the Gospels isn't the verse, but the **story**. You're learning the **stories** of the Resurrection.

You could break these into smaller "stories", if you liked. I've included small story headings where I would make these breaks.

But for our purposes, the story divisions don't really matter. We're repeating the whole thing each day. Story breaks are useful with a larger amount of material, because you can recite particular *stories* each day, rather than everything you've ever learned.

In the future, as you learn other texts, you can also recite entire chapters. Many chapters seem to break between stories.

You might think that single verses are easier to remember than whole stories. Verses are so much shorter! If you only wanted to remember one verse, this would be true. But since you're learning many verses, you'll find that they naturally snap together into stories.

Reciting in Different Ways

By now, you've recited these verses in different ways.

You've **read** them slowly, learning them for the first time, and using all the methods for speaking out, taking in, and imagining.

You've **reread** them, as you filled in the gaps of your memory.

You've gradually tried to **say them without looking**. When you've come to a tough patch, you've checked the words, to solidify your memory.

Sometimes I call this check a "rinse". At this stage, it feels like I'm slowly washing away the mud of my muddled forgetting, getting to the crystal clear memory beneath.

If you've been speaking the verses to friends or family members, you're already **telling the verses as stories**. No matter how much expression you use by yourself, speaking to others can bring out more. If you haven't told the verses to anyone yet, try it!

Or at least plan on trying it when you feel you've learned enough verses to tell a complete story.

Can you say the first few verses perfectly? If so, try a new way to recite them: **fast**. I've read more than one memorizer recommend that you say the words as quickly as you can.

Why fast? For one thing, it's different. Remember, different methods help strengthen your memories.

In my case, I find that speed can clear away some unnecessary hesitations. The extra effort helps me focus. I know these verses better than I think I do.

I used to think that a fast recitation was incompatible with imagining. Actually, no matter how fast you can talk, you can imagine faster.

But you have to be careful about speaking fast. You don't want to slip into a mindset of *rushing*, where you're trying to minimize your verse time as a "necessary evil."

Rushing, in fact, is the bane of happy learning.

Renewing Is Its Own Reward

It's extremely tempting to rush through recitations. But when we **rush**, we **defeat the whole purpose** of learning verses in the first place.

Rushing through your verses defeats the whole point of learning them.

Renewing the verses is its own reward.

Think about it. Why did you decide to learn the story of the Resurrection?

It's not a rhetorical question. Only you can say.

I do know that your goal includes knowing these verses by heart. But this actually gets rather complex. You want to *know* these verses so you can *think* with them, right? This can't just be a checkbox on a list of a thousand things to do before you die. You want to weave these words into your mind, so that your mind will move in *new thoughts*, thoughts you'd otherwise never have.

You may have other goals, too, like sharing the verses with your children or congregation. But whether you're interested in study or prayer (or both), I'm almost certain that you're hoping to *think differently* than you did before you started.

Here's the surprise. *You're already thinking differently*. Every time you renew these verses, *you're thinking about them.*

These new thoughts are not some distant goal that can only come when you've done the gruntwork of learning the verses. No. You've already arrived — as long as you don't rush.

Baking Cookies vs. Riding a Bike

This feels too abstract. Time to get concrete.

Think about making cookies. You do a whole bunch of weird rituals — breaking eggs, measuring pulverized grains, mixing in distilled herbs. You spread this gooey concoction onto a metal plate, and you put it into an oven. It's all quite bizarre. But at the end, if the magic works, you get to eat cookies.

Eating cookies is *nothing* like *baking* cookies. The two processes differ entirely. Most of us enjoy eating cookies. Enjoying the baking? That's an acquired taste. Some of us *endure* baking, for the sake of the cookies at the end.

Many goals in life share this same dynamic. If you want cookies, you have to bake them. If you want a house, you have to build it. If you want money, you have to work for it.

If you're lucky, you hunt for work you'll enjoy. But the work is still different from the mysterious magic of money.

This dynamic of work-then-reward gets burned into our brain. But not everything is like this

Think about riding a bike. When you first get onto a bike, you wobble and struggle and probably fall. But even so, you roll a few feet. You are practicing the *same* process that you hope to achieve.

One day, you'll ride so well that these early attempts will feel like another lifetime. And yet, you're *already biking*.

You can see this with kids. They don't say, "I want to go practice riding my bike, so that one day I can actually ride my bike." They want to *ride their bikes*, as well as they can, right now.

You're Already Thinking

If you're like me, you were first drawn to memorization as an exotic, foreign skill. You thought it would be like baking cookies. You would do all these arcane tricks, and then — ta-da! — you would relish the completely unrelated result.

But verses are like riding a bike. You're *already* thinking.

All the methods I'm showing you — Bible rhythms, daily renewal, imagining — they're simply different ways to *think* about these verses.

They aren't like baking, where you're not even supposed to taste the batter. No, you're already on the bike, already moving, already thinking.

You may have started out with a focus on *memorizing*, on the magic of getting the words perfect. That's still a worthy goal.

But memorizing is the *fruit* of thinking. Not the other way around.

Don't Waste Time "Memorizing"

I wasted a lot of time (a *lot*) trying to memorize things as "efficiently" as I could. I assumed that I wouldn't really think about the verses until after I'd memorized them.

This is precisely backwards. You start thinking about the verses right away, as soon as you read them. That's why we have books, to help us think. And you wean yourself off the training wheels of the book *by thinking*. You use these methods to *help you think* about the verses you've read.

Yes, it's grand when you can think so well that you no longer need the book. But this work depends entirely on the *quality of your thoughts*. You're not a hard drive. You're a thinker.

Don't think you need to "memorize" these verses first before you begin to enjoy new and exciting thoughts. **You're already thinking.**

Renewing Is Its Own Reward

I've talked about memorizing "efficiently". I used to think that "efficiency" meant "getting it over with as soon as possible."

Now I understand that, in memorization, "efficiency" means focusing on the methods that *help you think*.

Why does everyone hate rote repetition? Because it doesn't engage your thoughts. It feels like slave labor. You repeat words until you can't stand them any more. A few months later, if you don't renew them, you forget them anyway.

True, our time is limited. We have other responsibilities and desires besides learning the story of the Resurrection by heart. It is sensible to find "efficient" ways to memorize.

But when we use these methods, when we come to those times for saying verses, we need to *enter that time* as its *own reward*.

Learning these verses means that you have special times throughout the day when you think about Christ. Enjoy them.

Don't Watch the Clock

Most of the skills I'm teaching you are straightforward. You can learn to follow a sequence of simple steps.

But imagination is open-ended. One verse may instantly transport you to a vivid scene. With another, you may have to mull over it for several minutes.

I know I said that you only need to spend about fifteen minutes a day on this. But don't watch the clock. If you take an extra five or ten minutes to imagine well, good for you! Don't rush!

Rushing Wastes Time

If we *rush*, we're telling ourselves that this is just gruntwork. We're saying that we're not really doing anything worthwhile. We feel that we're simply paying in installments for a car we'll eventually get to drive.

This is sad. Instead of enjoying the time, instead of savoring the delights of imagination, we're snapping on our own shackles. We're making a little more of our day into dead, grumpy, time.

Even worse, we're also *messing up our memorization*. Rushing simply *doesn't work*.

Memorizing is a *complete experience*. You're connecting, remember? These verses will connect to *everything* that's happening to you while you think about them — including your emotions. If you always resent the time you spend on verses ... how much do you expect your mind to enjoy revisiting these memories? How strong do you think these memories will be?

"Saving time" by rushing only wastes all of it.

Renewing rewards you.

Rushing wastes your time.

Renew, Don't Review

Have you noticed that I try to say "renew" instead of "review"? Switching these words has been a paradigm shift for me.

"Review" conjures up all the worst parts of school:

- You're forced to do it. It's a chore.

- You review for the sake of some quiz or test, not the material itself.

- You're rehashing old stuff, in the same boring way.

But "renewing" feels totally different. We *renew* because we *want* to. You renew a friendship by calling up someone you love. You renew your strength every time you eat.

And renewing is *creative*. Another paradox: we memorize old words to lead us to new thoughts. Yes, we're also renewing the thoughts and connections we've already made. But you don't need to stop there. Renewing should be creative.

Renewing your memories is an act of *creativity*. You can think *new* thoughts every time you touch these verses.

Renewing is its own reward.

So don't hurry through renewal as one more task. Learn to savor your time with these verses.

A Beautiful, Old, Oral Translation

Learning to enjoy renewals can be a challenge. Here's another odd challenge to enjoy: the quirky old translation we're using. This old translation offers some surprising hidden features.

Why Use an Old Translation?

In case you haven't noticed, the translation you're memorizing is ... old. "Thees" and "thous" are liberally sprinkled throughout sentences that feel rather Shakespearean.

The language sounds strange. The rhythms are different. Occasionally, a word is completely foreign.

The reasons are simple. This is the Douay-Rheims Challoner translation. It was originally composed in the sixteenth and seventeenth centuries, then heavily revised in the eighteenth century. That's old. To our modern ears, the DRC is extremely similar to the more well-known King James Bible, also from the seventeenth century.

Almost every church you could attend will read a more modern translation. Why do I use this version?

Freedom

First, because this version is in the public domain.

I don't see the point of memorizing anything under copyright, at least not if you have a free option. We memorize to *recreate*. Copyright shackles this creativity.

True, you probably wouldn't get sued for repeating a copyrighted translation to your children. But freedom matters, and it begins in theory.

Almost all contemporary translations of the Bible are under copyright. Open any devotional book, and the small print will include a note explaining that the Bible verses are quoted with permission.

I appreciate the tremendous effort and expense that goes into translation. This is not the place to tackle the logistics of both claiming a text is Divine Revelation and then putting it under copyright. It's complicated.

Fortunately, a translation in the public domain neatly sidesteps all this. The public domain is free.

Oral Rhythms

The DRC also offers a surprise side benefit: **oral rhythms**.

In his major work *Orality and Literacy*, Walter J. Ong compares a passage from the Douay Old Testament (the seventeenth century version) to the same passage from the contemporary *New American Bible*.

We might think the Douay is different simply because it's "old". But Ong shows that the Douay is *oral*, "produced in a culture with a still massive oral residue."

This is huge.

Bible rhythms are critical to moving *beyond* reading, into *speaking* these verses. This quaint, arcane translation of the DRC is actually *better suited* to oral recitation than almost all contemporary translations.

In my memorizing, I've found two main aspects of the DRC that, although they distracted me at first, turned out to be helpful oral features.

The Opening "And"

Did your teacher ever tell you not to begin a sentence with "And"? Have you noticed that practically *every other verse* you've learned so far from the DRC begins with "And"? Why the difference?

As Ong explains, the use of "And" is *oral*. Think about how you tell a story. You naturally say, "We did this. And then we did this. Oh, and then that happened." We use those *connecting* words in the rhythm of speech.

When we *write*, we feel we have to *edit out* that part of the natural speech rhythm. Modern Bible translations use all sorts of variations on the opening "And". But in the original Greek, all those sentences really do begin with a word similar to "And".

These modern translations are meant to be *read*, not *spoken* and *heard*. Pick up a modern Bible, and read the verses you've learned so far *out loud*. Now say your DRC verses. Can you hear how all those repetitions of "And" sound more like natural speech?

Repetition

This leads to a larger difference between oral and written culture: **repetition**. Your teacher probably also taught you not to keep repeating the same word. If your character is *sad* at the beginning of the paragraph, he can't be *sad* again for awhile. He has to be *wistful* or *depressed* or *downcast*. Out comes the thesaurus.

Even for writing, this advice is problematic. For speech, it's fatal. In speaking, repetition is *essential*. Think about good speeches, or even commercials. They always repeat the essential points. Commercials cram the company name as many times into thirty seconds as is humanly possible. They say the phone number at least twice, if not three or four times. *Repetition makes you remember.*

Repetition can also stir *emotion*. The same word acquires stronger and stronger meaning, building like a wave.

When you see words or phrases repeated in the DRC, try not to mentally filter them out. When you speak them, the repetition will help you remember, and help you feel the rhythms.

What About Accuracy?

Yes, biblical scholarship has advanced since the eighteenth century. The DRC has the special disadvantage of being a "translation of a translation," since it's based on the Latin Vulgate (although they did consult the original Hebrew and Greek texts). Some spots are certainly less accurate than a contemporary translation.

However, translation isn't an exact science. For the stories we're learning, the differences from contemporary translations are more a matter of language than actual "errors".

Besides, don't forget the oral rhythms. We may lose some textual accuracy with the DRC, but we also gain back some oral rhythms.

Arcane Language

Arcane language can help or hinder. In many passages, the old language has a force and beauty that seems lost in most modern translations.

In other places, the sentence construction, or even the vocabulary, is just too foreign for me. I find myself adjusting the phrasing, as the forces of mental gravity tug the phrases into shapes more consistent with my internal laws of linguistic physics.

But it's still worth the effort to learn the text perfectly. Unless you want to mark the text with your edits, so you can see them, you should learn the text as it is written.

Could You Memorize a Modern Translation?

If you truly dislike this translation, you can always use the verse schedule and follow along in your own Bible. But you'll face a few challenges.

A modern Bible will cram everything into paragraph blocks, so you'll lose the critical *visual* reminders of rhythm that you'll find in this book.

Consider typing out the verses and breaking them into rhythmic lines. But don't share what you've typed with anyone, because a modern translation is probably under copyright. (A few translations are freely licensed.)

You may also though a modern translation has easier words, the more "bookish" rhythms are harder to remember.

Enjoy the DRC

I hope I've made the quirks of this translation a bit less mysterious. The DRC does take some getting used to.

The translation in this book is old, but the **oral rhythms** make it easier to remember than modern translations.

I have a dream to learn the original languages and make a new, freely licensed translation that uses modern language but is steeped in rhythms. Until then, oral overtones make the DRC a great choice for learning these stories by heart.

Move With the Rhythms

Here's another way to enter into these Bible rhythms: **moving**.

Remember Marcel Jousse, the French priest who wrote about Bible rhythms back in 1925? Jousse thought that speaking was not enough. You had to physically *move around*.

In his book, the *Oral Style*, a major theme is **gesture**. Jousse describes Middle Eastern schools where the children practically *danced* as they memorized texts.

Today, researchers into oral cultures still explore how people speak, move, and remember.

How can we use movement to memorize these texts? Honestly, I don't know yet. You tell me.

I'd love to move to these verses, but I haven't figured out how. When I try, the movement distracts me. Perhaps each rhythmic line would have to be much longer.

For me, movement in general has never been a strong suit. If you already love moving and dancing, why not try using these rhythms as you speak the verses? If you find a way to move to these verses, let me know! We could have a great new memory tool.

In some cultures, you **move** while you **memorize**. You can try swaying, stomping, or dancing to the rhythms as you speak.

The Palaces of Memory

If you've been learning one verse and reading one lesson per day, your daily set of verses is getting longer, isn't it? Have you surprised anyone yet with how much you know?

Saying a whole story may seem a bit magical. You can start with, "And on the first day of the week," and *keep going*. How could you do this?

In modern times, people are obsessed with computers. But in ancient cultures, that excitement was lavished on their own memories. In the fourth century, St. Augustine of Hippo wrote:

> And I come to the fields and spacious palaces of my memory, where are the treasures of innumerable images, brought into it ... by the senses....
>
> All these doth that great harbor of the memory receive in her numberless secret and inexpressible windings, to be forthcoming, and brought out at need; each entering in by his own gate, and there laid up.

> And though my tongue be still, and my throat mute, so can I sing as much as I will...
>
> I discern the breath of lilies from violets, though smelling nothing; and I prefer honey to sweet wine, smooth before rugged, at the time neither tasting nor handling, but remembering only.
>
> These things do I within, in that vast court of my memory. For there are present with me, heaven, earth, sea, and whatever I could think on ... besides what I have forgotten.
>
> There also meet I with myself, and recall myself, and when, where, and what I have done, and under what feelings....
>
> Great is this force of memory, excessive great, O my God; a large and boundless chamber! Who ever sounded the bottom thereof? Yet is this a power of mine, and belongs unto my nature; nor do I myself comprehend all that I am. Therefore is the mind too strait to contain itself....
>
> Great is the power of memory, a fearful thing, O my God, a deep and boundless manifoldness; and this thing is the mind, and this am I myself. What am I then, O my God? What nature am I? A life various and manifold, and exceeding immense.
>
> Behold in the plains, and caves, and caverns of my memory, innumerable and innumerably full of innumerable kinds of things ... over all these do I run, I fly; I dive on this side and on that, as far as I can, and there is no end.

You may have heard of the *Confessions of St. Augustine*, but you might not have known he was so enthusiastic about memory.

(You can read as much more as you like, for free, at gutenberg.org/etext/3296).

Our technology amazes us, but in the end, all our computers are only tools. Our minds will always dwarf their own dreams.

As you learn to remember deliberately, you may feel as if your own "palaces of memory" are slowly lighting up for the first time. Dark caves become shining terraces. Welcome to a new world.

What About Mnemonics?

When you read St. Augustine talk about the "palaces of memory", did it remind you of "memory palaces"? If you've read any memory books lately, you probably remembered this ancient memory trick.

You might be wondering if I'm ever going to get to the *real* "memory techniques". Everything we've learned so far may seem too natural, even simple. Well, here we are. The real memory technique is: don't use memory techniques.

Memory Swans and Palaces

Memory palaces, along with other memory tricks, are still fairly unknown in our culture. Lately, though, they've been slowly gaining in popularity. With the recent bestseller *Moonwalking With Einstein*, by Joshua Foer, as well as niche books by "gurus" like Tony Buzan and Dominic O'Brien, plus *Memorize Your Faith* by Kevin Vost, people in many circles are slowly discovering the quirky little world of mental tricks for memorizing.

These memory tricks boil down to two principles: *mnemonics* and *organizing* those mnemonics.

A *mnemonic* is a *memory prompt*, and it is (in theory) easy to remember. For instance, instead of memorizing the numeral "2", you memorize, say, a swan.

Why would you do this? A swimming swan with a bent neck looks a little like a "2". But a swan is also (in theory) easier and more fun to think about, and thus remember, than that stark, abstract number "2".

Once you make mnemonics, they must be carefully and cleverly *organized*. That lovely swan is no help if it flies off into the darkness of your mental "caves and caverns", and refuses to reappear when you need the third digit of your ATM pin.

The oldest known way to organize your mnemonics may be the "memory palace". Memory palaces date back at least to the ancient Greeks. First, you imagine a real place that you can remember easily, like your bedroom. Then, you imagine storing your mnemonics, in order, in definite spots around your bedroom. Your bed, your dresser, your desk, whatever.

That's it.

Why Mnemonics Do(n't) Work

Do memory palaces work? Sure. You remember the mnemonics, because when you think, "What did I store in my bed?" you magically *see* the mnemonic you put there. It's the same way you remember where you put *real* things, like your shoes or your jacket. You see a mental image of the thing in that spot. It's a brilliant hack, really.

Other organization methods include using "peg words", which are kind of like spots around a memory palace, except easier to forget, and also "chaining" mnemonics together, which is about what it sounds like, except that the chains tend to break.

Perhaps you sense a certain lack of enthusiasm on my part. Shouldn't I be more excited? Can't people store hundreds, thousands, *tens* of thousands of facts?

Kind of. They can store hundreds, thousands, and tens of thousands of *mnemonics*. But how much do they actually think about the things themselves?

The Wrong Way to Memorize the Bible

When I first found out about memory palaces, I got excited. So excited, that I eventually made up a separate mnemonic for every single verse in the Gospel of Mark. That's nearly *seven hundred* unique mnemonics.

As I memorized each verse, I stored the mnemonic in order around my in-laws' house. Each chapter got its own room. I started in the attic, and worked my way down and out to the backyard.

After several months, I had carefully stocked my mental model of that house with about seven hundred imaginary knick-knacks. In fact, I even had a system that let me locate the verse by the actual *number*. I'll spare you the details, but when I wanted a verse, I could navigate to the correct prompt almost every time.

Think about that. I had reliable, *random* access to almost seven hundred facts. If only I'd known about this back when I was earning grades instead of money.

The problem? The prompt instantly told me the *gist* of the verse, what it was about. But making the leap to the actual *words* of the verse didn't always quite work. At best, it took too much effort.

Mnemonic Mistakes

Slowly I realized that I had made three (at least) critical mistakes:

- I didn't believe I could form a clear mental picture of the actual words. Instead, I made a clear mental picture of the mnemonic.

- I postponed actually *thinking* about the verse. I thought I needed to "memorize" first, and get the bare words perfect. I planned to connect the words to rich imagination later. This was exactly backwards. I should have been visualizing *now*, while I spoke the words.

- I shattered the stories into isolated verses. Instead of renewing them together, as stories, I fed the verses separately into a system of randomized flashcards.

This isolation hamstrung my oral memory. I deftly *destroyed* all the oral memory aids that the original composers had carefully crafted: the rhythm, the context, the repetition of key words, and the sense of story, with a beginning, middle, and end. All gone. Exchanged for a bizarre visual prompt.

You Remember What You Think About

It's easy to see why I got confused. Visual mnemonics, especially bizarre ones (like moonwalking with Einstein), are easy to remember. So easy, it seems like we should just make mnemonics for everything, and our memory problems will be solved.

But memory prompts are just that — *prompts*. Prompts should kickstart the thinking you actually want to do. Your mind is designed for far more complexity than chuckling at distinguished physicists in spacesuits.

Here's the ultimate memory trick: **you remember what you think about.**

That's why sports fanatics can remember every score back to their great-grandfather. Film buffs can recite half a movie without even trying. All of us can recognize hundreds of corporate logos, just from navigating a modern landscape. And then there's our memory for songs...

True, we'll tend to forget mediocre athletes, boring movies and bland logos. If people want to be remembered, they have to make an effort. They need to be bright, colorful, exciting, unique, rhythmic, funny, dramatic, whatever. These qualities are precisely what make us more likely to think about them.

Revenge of the Prompts

In my case, I remember my in-laws' house, and hundreds of little knick-knacks. Actually, in many cases, the actual prompt has faded away, but I remember the *place* I had put it: the corner of the bathroom towel rack, the rings of the shower curtain, the bathroom faucet.

This makes sense. The place was real, and burned into my memory from being there. Plus, I had to focus on finding the *place* every time I searched for a verse. The place itself became my mnemonic.

Today, if I go too long without reviewing Mark, the actual words may start to blur. But almost every place can still trigger the *gist* of the verse.

Alas, this connection works both ways.

When I review the words of Mark, they automatically connect *back to these places*. I start the story of the demoniac and the pigs, and think of ... a towel rack.

When some people learn about making crazy mnemonics, they worry that these bizarre images will commandeer your brain. Don't worry. They don't take over, any more than the color of your library carpet, your first science fair project, or any of the other billion facts in your mind.

However, this gut fear is a shrewd intuition. You won't think of your crazy mnemonics all the time, but you might find you see them *whenever you recall the verses*. Through patient perseverance, I have expertly connected the possessed pigs to a towel rack.

As I relearn Mark as stories, I'm slowly making real scenes. But it's extra work. I should have baked these scenes into the words as I learned them the first time. Don't make the same mistake.

You remember what you think about.

Focus your energy on the actual words and thoughts you want to remember. Otherwise, you'll memorize prompts, not stories.

The Right Way (If Any) To Use a Memory Palace

Now you know why I waited so long to introduce you to memory palaces and the magical world of mnemonics. They're a powerful, seductive tool. But you have to know when to use them.

Is there *ever* a good time to use a memory palace? Perhaps.

Memory palaces excel at helping us organize abstract information into a *space*. You might use a palace as a *navigational* tool.

For instance, if you learn an entire Gospel, you might use one prompt for each story, or even each chapter. When one story doesn't naturally lead into the next, you could step back and check your prompts to see what comes next.

It seems that this light use wouldn't interfere with your experience of the verses. It could help you avoid skipping or switching stories, if you want to tell them in order.

But I can't be sure yet. It might be better to organize the material by focusing on the "starter phrases", as one author calls them, which begin each story or chapter.

At any rate, you won't need any palaces for the stories you're learning in this book. You'll find that each familiar incident flows naturally into the next.

Are Mnemonics Really That Bad?

It may seem that I've been unduly harsh on mnemonics. Many august intellectuals (including St. Thomas Aquinas) have sung their praises.

The danger, at least for me, has been that mnemonics have distracted me from thinking about the real things.

Of course, I say this as someone who has spent more time using mnemonics than 99.999% of the population. It's quite possible that mnemonics have strengthened my thinking in ways I don't yet realize and appreciate. And I'm sure that mnemonics will always have their uses.

But your mind is exceedingly, almost frighteningly suggestible. If you tell yourself, "I can't remember these words! I need a mnemonic," then you *won't* remember the words. But if you assure yourself that you *can* remember them, you *will*. It takes more than one look, but with practice, you will reach that goal. You will train that skill.

You may not believe in "positive thinking" making much of a difference in the real world. (Although, as you read the Gospels, you may start to wonder whether our modern concept of "positive thinking" overlaps with Christ's incessant insistence that our own "faith" makes us whole.)

But we aren't talking about the outside world. Memorizing happens *inside your head*. In your own head, you *do* make the rules. You either limit yourself, or you set goals and achieve them.

Mnemonics set the bar too low. You're capable of more.

Plus, they're extra work. Why divert your mental energy?

Finally, they're habit-forming. Mnemonics accustom you to thinking in a particular way. You get better at making mnemonics, not necessarily at real thinking.

For many reasons, it seems better to train yourself to observe and think about what you actually want to know. You can do it!

You've Learned How to Learn Verses!

Congratulations! You've learned how to memorize these verses. From now on, you can focus on the verses themselves.

I hope you've found a comfortable daily routine for your learning and recitations. If not, keep experimenting. You'll find a system that works.

Missed Days and "Deadlines"

If you miss a day (or two ... or three ...), don't give up! Pick up where you left off.

The twentieth and twenty-first chapters of John work out so that if you start on Easter Sunday and learn a verse each day, you'll finish right around Pentecost. But that doesn't mean you *have* to. If you miss days here and there, don't fret about going a bit past Pentecost before you finish.

If you really want to finish by Pentecost, you can learn an extra new verse each day until you catch up. But I wouldn't try this until after your first three or four weeks. It's so important not to rush.

Enjoy

Most important of all: *enjoy this*. Don't let learning the living, rhythmic Word of God slide into homework.

I know how easy it is to slip into the homework mindset. I still do it myself. Those are the times to stop and take a break. It's probably better to miss a day entirely than to "power through" with clenched teeth.

On the other hand, I've often experienced a certain inertia in getting started. Sometimes, I only need to say a few verses to get rolling. Then I enter that place of rhythm and imagination where I'm happy to recite.

Enjoy learning these verses!

If you're not in the mood, try to say a few verses anyway. You might slip into a happier place.

But after a few verses, if you're still grinding, stop. Take a break. Try again later.

There's only one more lesson. I suggest you wait to read it until you've learned all the verses in John 20 and 21.

God bless your Easter!

Keeping What You've Learned

You've done it.

You've memorized more than you ever thought possible. Verse by verse, day by day, week by week, you've laid up texts like treasures. Congratulations.

One task remains. Keep these treasures from slipping away.

First, Keep Repeating

By now, you've said the oldest verses over fifty times. You know them very, very well.

But the more recent verses are still fresh. You've only just now learned the last one.

Your first task is to cement the most recent verses. It may feel strange to keep reciting the Resurrection stories after the close of the Easter season, but if you don't, these stories will slip away. Each new verse needs to be repeated daily for about two weeks.

Two weeks is an estimate. If we were using "spaced repetition," you would have a complex schedule. But it's simpler to just repeat the last fourteen verses or so every day for two more weeks.

Then, Recite The Stories Once a Month

Meanwhile, get out your calendar for the next year. Mark **one day each month** (perhaps Sunday) to recite John 20 and 21. Write "Jn 20-21".

To make things easier, you can choose to recite each chapter on a different day instead.

Once a month will be more often than you need. But it's easy to schedule.

Make sure your first scheduled day is no more than a month from today. I don't want you to lose those last few verses.

If you ever get shaky on a story, simply repeat the whole story every day until you're confident again. When you've polished this memory, you can stop reciting it until your next monthly recitation.

Next year, you can probably say the stories every three months. After that, once or twice a year should be plenty. That's how spaced repetition works. Once you've done those frequent early repetitions, you can wait longer and longer as time goes on.

Ready for More?

Learn Christmas!

If you liked learning verses during Easter, why not celebrate Advent and Christmas by learning the Christmas stories? Consider *Christmas by Heart*, the next seasonal book in this series.

Since you've already trained your memory, you'll be able to learn **two verses a day** instead of one. (Not that you have to.)

As you keep learning verses, you can work your way up to three, four, or even five verses a day. Later books in this series will include special techniques for renewing these longer texts.

Use This Book Next Easter

You can also use this book again next Easter. You may choose to learn these verses all over again, renewing your memories with one or two new verses a day. Or, you may choose to learn one of the other Resurrection narratives, or the Pentecost narrative, at the back of this book.

Celebrate What You've Learned

Meanwhile, don't forget to celebrate what you've already done! You've acquired a new superpower! And you've used this power to write the stories of Christ in your heart.

Celebrating may sound cheesy. Embarrassing. But what's the alternative? If we don't savor our hard-won achievements, when will we ever enjoy anything?

So celebrate. You don't have to call the caterers, but you've already thought of something special even as we speak. Do it.

Keep in Touch

And let me know how all this went for you. I'd love to include your success story in future editions.

I'd also love **your feedback**. What worked for you? What didn't? As you know, I've developed this method through plenty of mistakes. I continue to search for more great improvements. The best ideas will come from people like you, who come to the task with fresh minds.

If you can leave your feedback as an **Amazon review**, you'll also help others find this book and learn what you've learned. These reviews make a huge difference.

I look forward to hearing your thoughts. Welcome to the club! Happy Easter!

Bill Powell
bill@howtoremember.biz
EasterByHeart.com

Other Resurrection Narratives

As promised, here are the Resurrection narratives from the other three Gospels.

This material can easily last you for several seasons of Easter! A warning, though: the Gospels are uniquely challenging because they can be so similar. If you learn John 20 and 21 first, these words will come to mind when you try to learn passages that are almost, but not quite, identical in another Gospel.

I wish I had an easy solution for this, but I don't. I'm still trying to figure out a clean way to avoid conflicting memories. I've considered various methods, such as singing each Gospel to a different tune. Or you could visualize each Gospel differently somehow, perhaps with a different set of "actors".

Learning four overlapping, similar and yet unique prose narratives may be one of the most challenging memory feats you can try!

For now, my best suggestion is to take it slow, and be patient with yourself. Focus on learning one Gospel at a time. You wouldn't try to learn Spanish and Italian at the same time, right? Don't try to learn Matthew until you're completely solid on John.

On the other hand, you will inevitably compare these narratives. It's fascinating to see which incidents occur only in one or two, and which occur in all four.

For instance, all four Resurrection stories begin with the women coming to the tomb. But only Matthew mentions the aftermath of the failed guards, only Luke gives the full story of Emmaus, and only John tells of Jesus making breakfast by the sea.

As you pay attention to these differences, you'll notice certain patterns within each evangelist. What do they tend to focus on? What do they leave out? These patterns may help you keep each narrative straight.

I love the idea of knowing all four versions of the Resurrection. But remember, there's no rush. Learning one version each Easter season will add up fast.

Matthew 28
Easter Morning
Matthew 28:1

Earthquake and angel

AND in the end
   of the sabbath,
when it began to dawn
   towards the first day
      of the week,
came Mary Magdalen
   and the other Mary,
      to see the sepulchre.

And behold
   there was a great earthquake.
For an angel of the Lord
   descended from heaven,
and coming,
   rolled back the stone,
      and sat upon it.

And his countenance was as lightning,
   and his raiment as snow.

And for fear of him,
   the guards were struck with terror,
      and became as dead men.

The angel speaks to the women

And the angel answering,
    said to the women:
Fear not you;
    for I know that you seek Jesus
        who was crucified.

He is not here,
    for he is risen,
        as he said.
Come,
    and see the place
        where the Lord was laid.

And going quickly,
    tell ye his disciples
        that he is risen:
and behold
    he will go before you into Galilee;
        there you shall see him.
Lo,
    I have foretold it to you.

Jesus meets the women

And they went out quickly from the sepulchre
    with fear and great joy,
        running to tell his disciples.

And behold Jesus met them,
    saying:
        All hail.
But they came up

and took hold of his feet,
    and adored him.

Then Jesus said to them:
    Fear not.
Go,
    tell my brethren
that they go into Galilee,
    there they shall see me.

After the Resurrection

Matthew 28:11

The story of the guards

Who when they were departed,
    behold some of the guards
        came into the city,
and told the chief priests
    all things that had been done.

And they being assembled
    together with the ancients,
taking counsel,
    gave a great sum of money
        to the soldiers,

Saying:
    Say you,
        His disciples came by night,
and stole him away
    when we were asleep.

And if the governor shall hear this,
  we will persuade him,
    and secure you.

So they taking the money,
  did as they were taught:
and this word was spread abroad
  among the Jews
    even unto this day.

The disciples meet Jesus on the mountain

And the eleven disciples
  went into Galilee,
unto the mountain
  where Jesus had appointed them.

And seeing them they adored:
  but some doubted.

And Jesus coming,
  spoke to them,
saying:
  All power is given to me
    in heaven and in earth.

Going therefore,
  teach ye all nations;
baptizing them in the name of the Father,
  and of the Son,
    and of the Holy Ghost.

Teaching them to observe all things whatsoever
  I have commanded you:

and behold I am with you all days,
    even to the consummation
        of the world.

Mark 16
Resurrection
Mark 16:1

Women come to the sepulchre

And when the sabbath was past,
    Mary Magdalen
        and Mary the mother of James and Salome
bought sweet spices,
    that coming,
        they might anoint Jesus.

And very early in the morning,
    the first day of the week,
they come to the sepulchre,
    the sun being now risen.

And they said one to another:
    Who shall roll us back the stone
        from the door of the sepulchre?

And looking,
    they saw the stone rolled back.
        For it was very great.

An angel speaks to the women

And entering into the sepulchre,
    they saw a young man
sitting on the right side,
    clothed with a white robe:
        and they were astonished.

Who saith to them:
    Be not affrighted.
You seek Jesus of Nazareth,
    who was crucified.
He is risen:
    he is not here.
Behold
    the place where they laid him.

But go,
    tell his disciples and Peter
that he goeth before you
    into Galilee.
There you shall see him,
    as he told you.

Women flee, but Jesus appears

But they going out,
    fled from the sepulchre:
for a trembling and fear
    had seized them.
And they said nothing to any man:
    for they were afraid.

But he rising early
    the first day of the week,
appeared first to Mary Magdalen;
    out of whom he had cast seven devils.

After the Resurrection

Mark 16:10

Apostles don't believe

She went and told them
    that had been with him,
        who were mourning and weeping.

And they hearing that he was alive
    and had been seen by her,
        did not believe.

And after that he appeared
    in another shape
        to two of them walking,
as they were going
    into the country.

And they going told it to the rest:
    neither did they believe them.

Final words of Jesus

At length he appeared to the eleven
    as they were at table:
and he upbraided them
    with their incredulity

and hardness of heart,
because they did not believe
them who had seen him
after he was risen again.

And he said to them:
Go ye into the whole world
and preach the gospel
to every creature.

He that believeth and is baptized
shall be saved:
but he that believeth not
shall be condemned.

And these signs shall follow
them that believe:
In my name they shall cast out devils.
They shall speak with new tongues.

They shall take up serpents:
and if they shall drink any deadly thing,
it shall not hurt them.
They shall lay their hand upon the sick:
and they shall recover.

And the Lord Jesus,
after he had spoken to them,
was taken up into heaven
and sitteth on the right hand of God.

But they going forth
preached every where:
the Lord working withal,
and confirming the word
with signs that followed.

Luke 24
Easter Morning
Luke 24:1

Women at the tomb

AND on the first day of the week,
    very early in the morning,
they came to the sepulchre,
    bringing the spices
        which they had prepared.

And they found the stone
    rolled back from the sepulchre.

And going in,
    they found not the body
        of the Lord Jesus.

And it came to pass,
    as they were astonished
        in their mind at this,
behold,
    two men stood by them,
        in shining apparel.

And as they were afraid,
    and bowed down their countenance
        towards the ground,
they said unto them:
    Why seek you the living
        with the dead?

He is not here,
    but is risen.
Remember how he spoke unto you,
    when he was in Galilee,

Saying:
    The Son of man must be delivered
        into the hands of sinful men,
and be crucified,
    and the third day rise again.

And they remembered
    his words.

The women tell the disciples

And going back from the sepulchre,
    they told all these things to the eleven,
        and to all the rest.

And it was Mary Magdalen,
    and Joanna,
        and Mary of James,
and the other women
    that were with them,
who told these things
    to the apostles.

And these words seemed to them
    as idle tales;
        and they did not believe them.

But Peter rising up,
    ran to the sepulchre,

and stooping down,
   he saw the linen cloths
      laid by themselves;
and went away wondering in himself
   at that which was come to pass.

Emmaus

Luke 24:13

Two disciples leave for Emmaus

And behold,
   two of them went,
      the same day,
to a town
   which was sixty furlongs from Jerusalem,
      named Emmaus.

And they talked together
   of all these things
      which had happened.

Jesus meets them on the road

And it came to pass,
   that while they talked
      and reasoned with themselves,
Jesus himself also drawing near,
   went with them.

But their eyes were held,
   that they should not know him.

And he said to them:
    What are these discourses
that you hold one with another
    as you walk,
        and are sad?

Cleophas: "We hoped that it was he..."

And the one of them,
    whose name was Cleophas,
answering,
    said to him:
Art thou only a stranger
    to Jerusalem,
and hast not known the things
    that have been done there
        in these days?

To whom he said:
    What things?
And they said:
    Concerning Jesus of Nazareth,
        who was a prophet,
mighty in work and word
    before God and all the people;

And how our chief priests and princes
    delivered him to be condemned to death,
        and crucified him.

But we hoped,
    that it was he
        that should have redeemed Israel:
and now besides all this,

today is the third day
    since these things were done.

Cleophas tells Jesus of the Resurrection

Yea and certain women also
    of our company
        affrighted us,
who before it was light,
    were at the sepulchre,

And not finding his body,
    came, saying,
that they had also seen
    a vision of angels,
        who say that he is alive.

And some of our people
    went to the sepulchre,
and found it so
    as the women had said,
        but him they found not.

Jesus expounds the scriptures

Then he said to them:
    O foolish, and slow of heart
to believe in all things
    which the prophets have spoken.

Ought not Christ
    to have suffered these things,
        and so to enter into his glory?

And beginning at Moses
    and all the prophets,
he expounded to them
    in all the scriptures,
        the things that were concerning him.

Jesus breaks bread at Emmaus

And they drew night to the town,
    whither they were going:
and he made as though
    he would go farther.

But they constrained him;
    saying:
Stay with us,
    because it is towards evening,
        and the day is now far spent.
            And he went in with them.

And it came to pass,
    whilst he was at table with them,
he took bread,
    and blessed,
        and brake,
            and gave to them.

And their eyes were opened,
    and they knew him:
and he vanished
    out of their sight.

And they said
    one to the other:

Was not our heart
   burning within us,
whilst he spoke in this way,
   and opened to us the scriptures?

Jesus in the Upper Room

Luke 24:33

"Peace be to you"

And rising up,
   the same hour,
      they went back to Jerusalem:
and they found the eleven
   gathered together,
      and those that were staying with them,

Saying:
   The Lord is risen indeed,
      and hath appeared to Simon.

And they told what things
   were done in the way;
and how they knew him
   in the breaking of the bread.

Now whilst they were speaking these things,
   Jesus stood in the midst of them,
      and saith to them:
Peace be to you;
   it is I,
      fear not.

But they being troubled and frightened,
    supposed that they saw a spirit.

Jesus has flesh and bones

And he said to them:
    Why are you troubled,
and why do thoughts
    arise in your hearts?

See my hands and feet,
    that it is I myself;
handle,
    and see:
for a spirit hath not flesh and bones,
    as you see me to have.

And when he had said this,
    he shewed them his hands and feet.

But while they yet believed not,
    and wondered for joy,
he said:
    Have you any thing to eat?

And they offered him a piece
    of a broiled fish,
        and a honeycomb.

And when he had eaten before them,
    taking the remains,
        he gave to them.

Jesus opens their understanding

And he said to them:
    These are the words
which I spoke to you,
    while I was yet with you,
that all things
    must needs be fulfilled,
which are written in the law of Moses,
    and in the prophets,
        and in the psalms,
            concerning me.

Then he opened their understanding,
    that they might understand
        the scriptures.

And he said to them:
    Thus it is written,
and thus it behoved Christ to suffer,
    and to rise again from the dead,
        the third day:

And that penance and remission of sins
    should be preached in his name,
unto all nations,
    beginning at Jerusalem.

And you are witnesses
    of these things.

And I send the promise
    of my Father upon you:
but stay you in the city

till you be endued
    with power from on high.

Jesus ascends to Heaven

And he led them out
    as far as Bethania:
and lifting up his hands,
    he blessed them.

And it came to pass,
    whilst he blessed them,
he departed from them,
    and was carried up to heaven.

And they adoring
    went back into Jerusalem
        with great joy.

And they were always in the temple,
    praising and blessing God.
        Amen.

Acts 1
Jesus Ascends Into Heaven
Acts 1:1

Jesus stays with the disciples forty days

THE former treatise I made,
    O Theophilus,
of all things which Jesus began
    to do and to teach,

Until the day on which,
    giving commandments
        by the Holy Ghost
to the apostles
    whom he had chosen,
        he was taken up.

To whom also he shewed himself
    alive after his passion,
        by many proofs,
for forty days appearing to them,
    and speaking of the kingdom of God.

Final conversation with the disciples

And eating together with them,
    he commanded them,
that they should not depart
    from Jerusalem,
but should wait for the promise
    of the Father,
which you have heard

(saith he)
    by my mouth.

For John indeed baptized with water,
    but you shall be baptized
        with the Holy Ghost,
            not many days hence.

They therefore who were come together,
    asked him,
        saying:
Lord,
    wilt thou at this time
        restore again the kingdom to Israel?

But he said to them:
    It is not for you to know
        the times or moments,
which the Father hath put
    in his own power:

But you shall receive the power
    of the Holy Ghost coming upon you,
and you shall be witnesses unto me
    in Jerusalem,
and in all Judea,
    and Samaria,
and even to the uttermost part
    of the earth.

Jesus ascends into Heaven

And when he had said these things,
>   while they looked on,
>>   he was raised up:
and a cloud received him
>   out of their sight.

And while they were beholding him
>   going up to heaven,
behold two men stood by them
>   in white garments.

Who also said:
>   Ye men of Galilee,
why stand you looking
>   up to heaven?
This Jesus who is taken up
>   from you into heaven,
shall so come,
>   as you have seen him
>>   going into heaven.

Matthias Becomes an Apostle

Acts 1:12

Praying in the upper room

Then they returned to Jerusalem
>   from the mount that is called Olivet,
which is nigh Jerusalem,
>   within a sabbath day's journey.

And when they were come in,
    they went up into an upper room,
where abode Peter and John,
    James and Andrew,
Philip and Thomas,
    Bartholomew and Matthew,
James of Alpheus,
    and Simon Zelotes,
and Jude the brother
    of James.

All these were persevering with one mind
    in prayer with the women,
and Mary the mother of Jesus,
    and with his brethren.

Peter rises in the midst of the brethren

In those days
    Peter rising up in the midst
        of the brethren, said:
(now the number of persons together
    was about an hundred and twenty:)

Men, brethren,
    the scripture must needs be fulfilled,
which the Holy Ghost spoke before
    by the mouth of David
        concerning Judas,
who was the leader of them
    that apprehended Jesus:

Who was numbered with us,
    and had obtained part of this ministry.

The death of Judas

And he indeed hath possessed a field
    of the reward of iniquity,
and being hanged,
    burst asunder in the midst:
        and all his bowels gushed out.

And it became known
    to all the inhabitants of Jerusalem:
so that the same field was called
    in their tongue,
        Haceldama,
that is to say,
    The field of blood.

For it is written
    in the book of Psalms:
Let their habitation become desolate,
    and let there be none to dwell therein.
And his bishopric
    let another take.

Matthias is chosen as the new apostle

Wherefore of these men
    who have companied with us all the time
that the Lord Jesus came in
    and went out among us,

Beginning from the baptism of John,
    until the day wherein
        he was taken up from us,
one of these must be made a witness with us

of his resurrection.

And they appointed two,
    Joseph, called Barsabas,
        who was surnamed Justus,
            and Matthias.

And praying,
    they said:
Thou, Lord,
    who knowest the hearts of all men,
shew whether of these two
    thou hast chosen,

To take the place
    of this ministry and apostleship,
from which Judas hath by transgression fallen,
    that he might go to his own place.

And they gave them lots,
    and the lot fell upon Matthias,
and he was numbered
    with the eleven apostles.

Acts 2
Wind and Tongues

Acts 2:1

The Holy Spirit descends in a mighty wind

AND when the days of the Pentecost
    were accomplished,
they were all together
    in one place:

And suddenly there came
    a sound from heaven,
        as of a mighty wind coming,
and it filled the whole house
    where they were sitting.

And there appeared to them
    parted tongues
        as it were of fire,
and it sat
    upon every one of them:

And they were all filled
    with the Holy Ghost,
and they began to speak
    with divers tongues,
according as the Holy Ghost
    gave them to speak.

Jews of all nations understand them

Now there were dwelling at Jerusalem,
    Jews, devout men,
        out of every nation under heaven.

And when this was noised abroad,
    the multitude came together,
        and were confounded in mind,
because that every man heard them speak
    in his own tongue.

And they were all amazed,
    and wondered,
        saying:
Behold, are not all these,
    that speak,
        Galileans?

And how have we heard,
    every man our own tongue
        wherein we were born?

Parthians,
    and Medes,
        and Elamites,
and inhabitants of Mesopotamia,
    Judea,
        and Cappadocia,
Pontus and Asia,
    Phrygia,
        and Pamphylia,
Egypt,
    and the parts of Libya about Cyrene,

and strangers of Rome,

Jews also,
    and proselytes,
Cretes,
    and Arabians:
we have heard them speak
    in our own tongues
        the wonderful works of God.

And they were all astonished,
    and wondered,
saying one to another:
    What meaneth this?

But others mocking, said:
    These men are full of new wine.

Peter Preaches

Acts 2:14

"I will pour out of my Spirit upon all flesh"

But Peter standing up with the eleven,
    lifted up his voice,
        and spoke to them:
Ye men of Judea,
    and all you that dwell in Jerusalem,
be this known to you,
    and with your ears
        receive my words.

For these are not drunk,
    as you suppose,
seeing it is
    but the third hour of the day:

But this is that which was spoken of
    by the prophet Joel:

And it shall come to pass,
    in the last days,
        (saith the Lord,)
I will pour out of my Spirit
    upon all flesh:
and your sons and your daughters shall prophesy,
    and your young men shall see visions,
        and your old men shall dream dreams.

And upon my servants indeed,
    and upon my handmaids
will I pour out in those days
    of my spirit,
        and they shall prophesy.

Signs in the heavens

And I will shew wonders in the heaven above,
    and signs on the earth beneath:
blood and fire,
    and vapour of smoke.

The sun shall be turned into darkness,
    and the moon into blood,
before the great and manifest
    day of the Lord come.

And it shall come to pass,
    that whosoever shall call
        upon the name of the Lord,
            shall be saved.

Jesus, crucified and risen

Ye men of Israel,
    hear these words:
Jesus of Nazareth,
    a man approved of God among you,
by miracles,
    and wonders,
        and signs,
which God did by him,
    in the midst of you,
        as you also know:

This same being delivered up,
    by the determinate counsel
        and foreknowledge of God,
you by the hands of wicked men
    have crucified and slain.

Whom God hath raised up,
    having loosed the sorrows of hell,
as it was impossible
    that he should be holden by it.

David prophesied about Jesus

For David saith concerning him:
    I foresaw the Lord before my face:
because he is at my right hand,

that I may not be moved.

For this my heart hath been glad,
    and any tongue hath rejoiced:
moreover my flesh also
    shall rest in hope.

Because thou wilt not leave
    my soul in hell,
nor suffer thy Holy One
    to see corruption.

Thou hast made known to me
    the ways of life:
thou shalt make me full of joy
    with thy countenance.

David died, but Christ rose

Ye men, brethren,
    let me freely speak to you
        of the patriarch David;
that he died,
    and was buried;
and his sepulchre is with us
    to this present day.

Whereas therefore he was a prophet,
    and knew that God hath sworn to him
        with an oath,
that of the fruit of his loins
    one should sit upon his throne.

Foreseeing this, he spoke
      of the resurrection of Christ.
For neither was he left in hell,
      neither did his flesh see corruption.

This Jesus hath God raised again,
      whereof all we are witnesses.

Jesus is Lord

Being exalted therefore
      by the right hand of God,
and having received of the Father
      the promise of the Holy Ghost,
he hath poured forth this
      which you see and hear.

For David ascended not into heaven;
      but he himself said:
The Lord said to my Lord,
      sit thou on my right hand,

Until I make thy enemies
      thy footstool.

Therefore let all the house of Israel
      know most certainly,
that God hath made
      both Lord and Christ,
this same Jesus,
      whom you have crucified.

The Multitude Seeks Baptism
Acts 2:37

Do penance and be baptized

Now when they had heard these things,
    they had compunction in their heart,
and said to Peter,
    and to the rest of the apostles:
What shall we do,
    men and brethren?

But Peter said to them:
    Do penance,
and be baptized every one of you
    in the name of Jesus Christ,
        for the remission of your sins:
and you shall receive
    the gift of the Holy Ghost.

For the promise is to you,
    and to your children,
        and to all that are far off,
whomsoever the Lord our God
    shall call.

And with very many other words
    did he testify and exhort them, saying:
Save yourselves
    from this perverse generation.

Three thousand new Christians

They therefore that received his word,
    were baptized;
and there were added in that day
    about three thousand souls.

And they were persevering
    in the doctrine of the apostles,
and in the communication
    of the breaking of bread,
        and in prayers.

And fear came
    upon every soul:
many wonders also
    and signs were done
        by the apostles in Jerusalem,
and there was great fear
    in all.

The early Christians in Jerusalem

And all they that believed,
    were together,
        and had all things common.

Their possessions and goods they sold,
    and divided them to all,
        according as every one had need.

And continuing daily with one accord
    in the temple,
and breaking bread
    from house to house,
they took their meat with gladness
    and simplicity of heart;

Praising God,
    and having favour
      with all the people.
And the Lord increased daily together
    such as should be saved.

Let Me Know

If you decide to learn one of these other narratives, please let me know how it goes! I'm always looking for fresh ideas.

Bill Powell
bill@howtoremember.biz
EasterByHeart.com

About the Author

Bill Powell has memorized tens of thousands of words, including the entire Gospel of Mark. He explores new ways to think, imagine and remember at **HowToRemember.biz**.

Bill lives in Virginia, in the Shenandoah Valley, with his wife, their four children, and a young forest garden.

Ready to Learn More?

You've learned the Resurrection. Now keep learning with the **Books by Heart**™ series.

Christmas by Heart

This book offers you an exciting new Advent and Christmas ritual: a daily Christmas verse. Every day, you'll learn a new verse of the Christmas story.

These verses will add up. By the end of the seasons, you'll know *every* Christmas verse we have in the Gospels. And you will have celebrated the *seasons* of Advent and Christmas.

Read more at **ChristmasByHeart.com**.

Lent by Heart

This Lent, learn the **Passion stories of Mark 15**.

You don't have to choose a Lenten sacrifice, and then *also* figure out some way to "enter more deeply into the season". When you learn the Passion by heart, you think about Christ every single day.

Read more at **LentByHeart.com**.

BooksByHeart.com

BLUE VINE

.